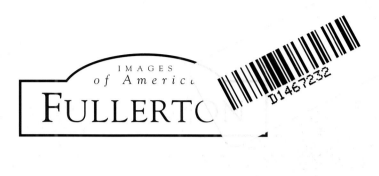
IMAGES
of America

FULLERTON

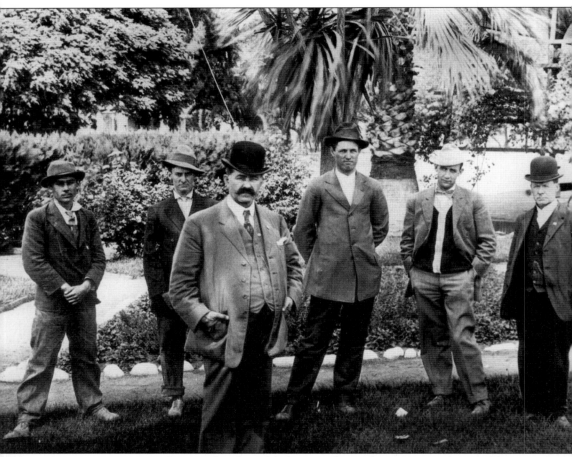

In 1904, Santa Fe Park opened and quickly became *the* outdoor meeting place and hangout for locals, including these dandies. Fullerton did not have a park commission until 1914, so in May 1908 the city marshall was instructed to oversee the park and its visitors at no extra cost to the city. Santa Fe Park, Fullerton's first park, was located at the corner of Santa Fe and Spadra Road.

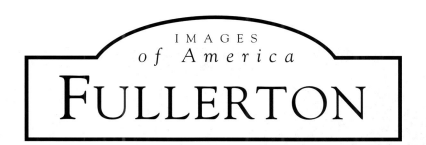

IMAGES
of America

FULLERTON

Fullerton Public Library

Kathy Morris
Debora Richey
Cathy Thomas

ARCADIA

Published by Arcadia Publishing
Charleston SC, Chicago IL, Portsmouth NH, San Francisco CA

Printed in Great Britain

Library of Congress Catalog Card Number: 2004110514

For all general information contact Arcadia Publishing at:
Telephone 843-853-2070
Fax 843-853-0044
E-mail sales@arcadiapublishing.com
For customer service and orders:
Toll-Free 1-888-313-2665

Visit us on the internet at http://www.arcadiapublishing.com

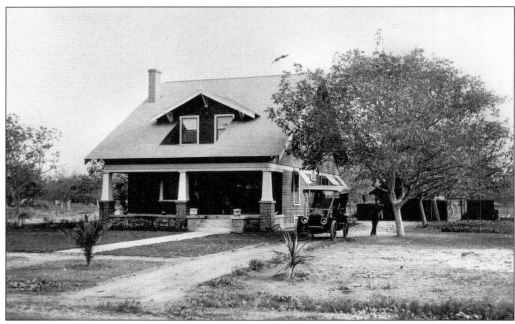

In this photo, F.W. Wood stands next to his automobile and ranch home on South Spadra Road in 1911. Wood was a chicken rancher.

CONTENTS

ACKNOWLEDGMENTS

While researching and compiling the photographs for this pictorial history of Fullerton, the authors relied greatly on the support, research, and technical expertise of many individuals. We would like to thank Joanne Hardy and Sharon Perry for all their generosity, patience, and support during the entire six-month process. In writing the captions, we relied on previous research completed by three local historians: Bob Linnell (*Fullerton Through the Years: A Survey of Architectural, Cultural & Environmental Heritage*), Bob Ziebell (*Fullerton: A Pictorial History*), and Evelyn Cadman (*Images of Yesterday: Fullerton Photo Album*). Their extensive expert research on Fullerton saved us hours of time. We also relied on the photographs and other materials collected and processed by earlier archivists of the local history room of the Fullerton Public Library—Kathryn Smith, Evelyn Cadman, and Jane Mueller—and we would like to thank these librarians for the development of this premier historical collection. We would also like to thank the following individuals for their technical expertise: Jim Powell, Kyle Samudio, and Eva Bird.

The purpose of this book is to celebrate Fullerton's centennial and to highlight the photography collection housed in the Launer Room of the Fullerton Public Library. All of the photographs for this book were taken from the Launer Room, which has the most extensive collection of current and historical photographs in the city. Because of space limitations, only a very small selection of photographs from this invaluable collection were used, and the authors hope that this book will encourage interested readers to visit the Launer Room for more information about Fullerton's rich and diverse history.

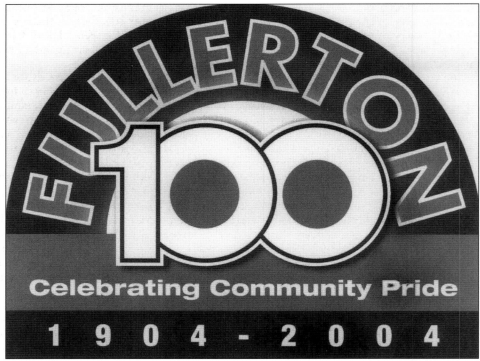

Fullerton's centennial logo, celebrating the city's incorporation in 1904, was designed by Michael Hofeldt, senior graphic designer at California State University, Fullerton.

INTRODUCTION

"The most desolate, lonesome place in the world" is how Maria Bastanchury described Fullerton to a friend after moving to Southern California with her new husband in 1864. There were only two homes between her and Los Angeles, and she was the only woman in the area. If she were alive today, Mrs. Bastanchury would be amazed at the changes the now bustling city has undergone.

In 1887, two brothers from Malden, Massachusetts—George and Edward Amerige—started it all. While hunting quail and dove near Anaheim while on vacation, they became interested in the area of land that is now Fullerton and decided to develop a town. The two brothers, former grain merchants, purchased 430 acres for approximately $68,000, and on July 5, 1887, Edward Amerige drove the first survey stake for the townsite of Fullerton in a field of mustard at what is now the intersection of Harbor Boulevard and Commonwealth Avenue. The town's future was secured when the Amerige brothers were able to convince George H. Fullerton, president of the Pacific Land and Improvement Company—the development arm of the Santa Fe Railroad—to route the railroad through the fledgling town.

During its first years, Fullerton was a typical western town. Railroad construction brought a rough and undesirable element, and early settlers often told of gunfights in saloons. On the heels of construction crews, however, came the backbone of the community—families. And with the families came the stabilizing influence of homes, churches, schools, banks, and libraries.

Agriculture quickly became the new community's leading industry, with Fullerton packinghouses shipping as much as $15 million in citrus crops in a banner year. At one time, Fullerton boasted more orange groves than any other Orange County city. Oil was discovered in 1890, and this black gold provided much needed revenue for city coffers. The oil boom continued through the 1920s, leading to a continuing influx of new residents, many of them immigrants, and to the establishment of middle-class neighborhoods.

By applying for and receiving federal relief aid in record numbers, Fullerton residents were able to weather the Great Depression of the 1930s. The city's last big boom period began in the late 1940s as veterans returning from World War II began demanding homes for their families. In 1948 permit valuations reached $2.5 million and, in 1949, set a record $3.2 million, which more than doubled in 1950. In 1956, the building permit valuation skyrocketed to $114 million. The southeast industrial area was established as a manufacturing zone, and before the 1950s had ended, the city had 142 industries producing a variety of goods.

By the 1970s, the rapid growth that characterized postwar Fullerton had slowed considerably. The city was now able to concentrate on providing the amenities all these new families and businesses demanded. New libraries and schools were built, a cultural center and a museum were opened, parks and community centers were developed, recreational trails were provided, and human service programs were instituted. Educational opportunities also blossomed. Fullerton College, established in 1913 with only 28 students, was joined by California State University, Fullerton, Western State University College of Law, Pacific Christian College, and the Southern California College of Optometry. Fullerton now boasts over 130,000 residents, 10,630 businesses, and 45,537 housing units within its 22.3 square miles.

The images in this book, many never seen before, highlight the individuals, events, businesses, and social life of Fullerton since its founding in 1887. The photographs represent only a small part of the rich historic past of this once small town, now one of the major cities in Orange County. As Fullertonians honor the 100-year anniversary of the city's incorporation, there is much to be proud of and to celebrate.

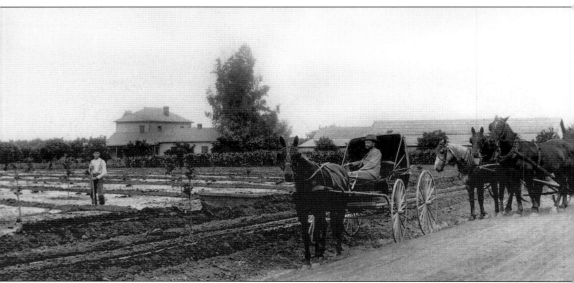

Financier William F. Botsford sits in a buggy on his ranch and winery in East Fullerton in 1891. Botsford, who spent most of his time in Los Angeles, was the president of banks and oil companies and also owned 280 acres in Placentia. In 1896 a disgruntled employee started a destructive fire on the property, considered at the time to be the largest fire in county history.

One
FOUNDERS, PIONEERS, VISITORS, AND CELEBRITIES

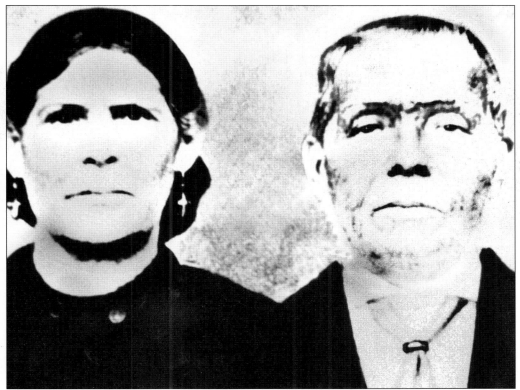

Maria and Juan Pacifico Ontiveros were owners of the 35,000-acre Rancho San Juan Cajon de Santa Ana, an 1833 land grant that eventually became the cities of Fullerton, Anaheim, Brea, and Placentia. Pacifico, a former soldier and overseer of Mission San Juan Capistrano, married María Martina Osuña of Santa Barbara on November 25, 1825. The couple had 13 children, and the family line still continues in Fullerton.

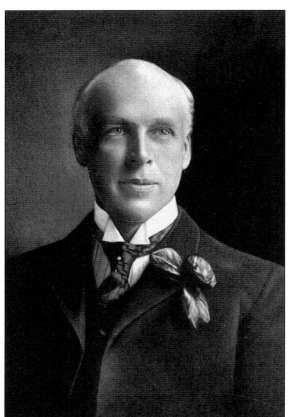

Edward R. Amerige (1857–1915) and his brother George came to San Francisco from Malden, Massachusetts for a vacation and were persuaded to visit the southern part of the state for the winter to hunt in the marshes near Westminster. While hunting quail and dove near the Anaheim area where they had been staying, they became interested in the land that is now Fullerton and decided to start a town.

In 1887, the Amerige brothers hired a Los Angeles photographer to create a real estate promotional sales book of Fullerton scenes. Taken from *Views of Fullerton*, this image shows George Amerige (1855–1947) in a buggy in what is now downtown Fullerton. The small building in the background is the Amerige Brothers Real Estate Office, which has been preserved in Amerige Park.

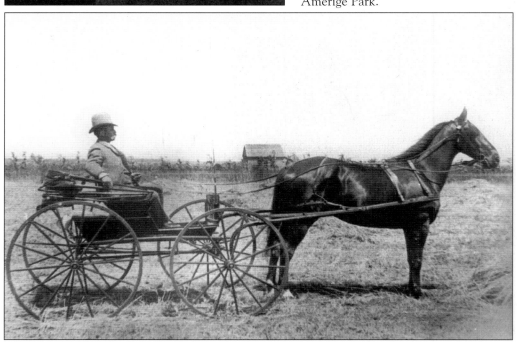

George H. Fullerton (1853–1929), president of the Pacific Land and Improvement Company, the development arm of the Santa Fe Railroad, was instrumental in having the railroad routed through the fledgling town. In appreciation, the town was named after him, even though he left the area the same year that the town was founded.

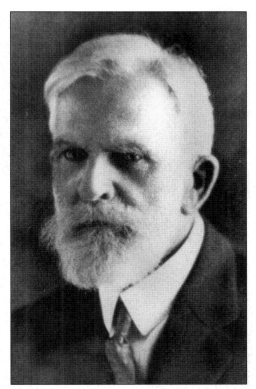

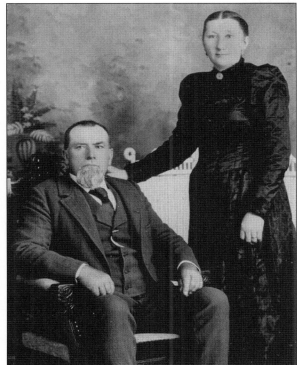

In 1872 dairy farmer Henry T. Hetebrink Sr.—shown here with his wife, Rebecka—loaded the cattle from his Northern California ranch onto a boat. Docking at Anaheim Landing (now Seal Beach), Hetebrink drove the cattle across Orange County until reaching what is now the California State University, Fullerton campus. The Hetebrinks' brick home (1886) still stands on the campus.

11

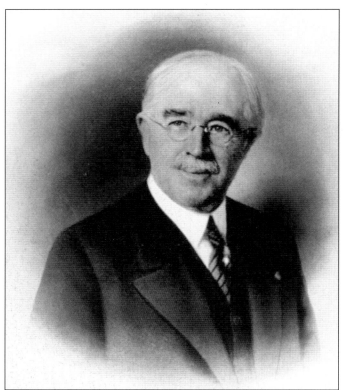

Charles C. Chapman's innovative production and marketing methods helped establish the Valencia orange as a highly successful Southern California industry, prompting the title "Father of the Valencia Orange Industry." Chapman (1853–1944), who served as Fullerton's first mayor, declined President Calvin Coolidge's offer to serve as his running mate in 1925.

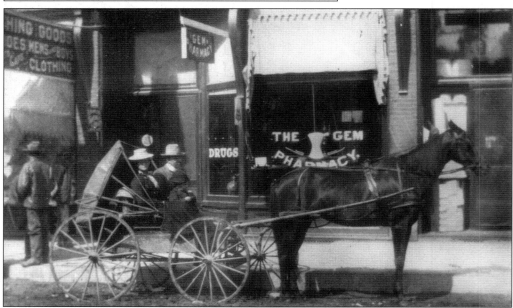

In 1888, Flora and William Starbuck came to town and opened the first drugstore, the Gem Pharmacy, in the 100 block of East Commonwealth. The store, shown here in 1900, also housed Fullerton's first library. It was demolished to make way for the Odd Fellows Temple (1927), which is now the Williams Building.

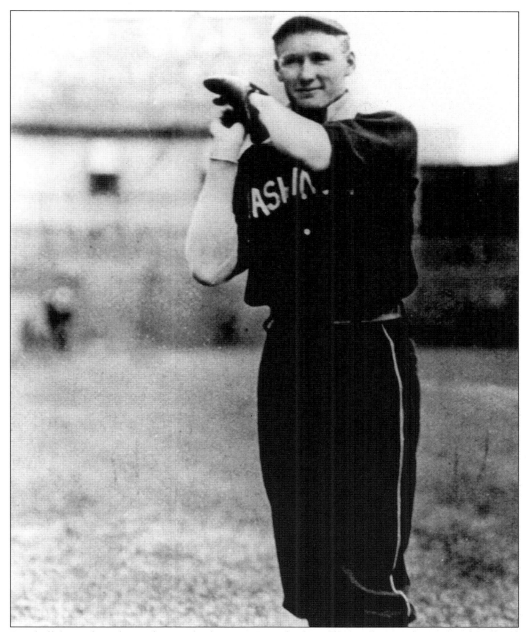

Baseball legend Walter Johnson ("The Big Train") played for Fullerton Union High School before moving up to the Washington Nationals (later renamed the Senators) in 1907, where he was their star pitcher for an astounding two decades. Along with what is reputed to be the greatest fastball in history, Johnson was so admired for his sportsmanship that fans would root for him against their own teams. Johnson and Honus Wagner were among the five original inductees into the Baseball Hall of Fame in 1936. FUHS is the only high school to produce three ballplayers who pitched no hitters in the major leagues: Johnson, Steve Busby (Kansas City Royals), and Mike Warren (Oakland As). (Photo courtesy of the Cooperstown National Baseball Hall of Fame.)

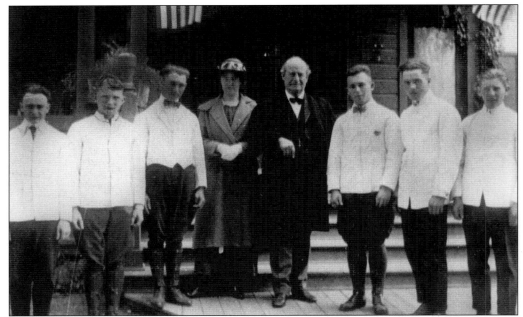

Famous orator, presidential candidate, and Scopes Trial lawyer William Jennings Bryan (1860–1927) visited Fullerton on May 14, 1917. Students from the high school cooking class had prepared a three-course breakfast for the famous speaker. After posing for this picture in front of the Hotel Shay (formerly the St. George Hotel), Bryan addressed the high school student body.

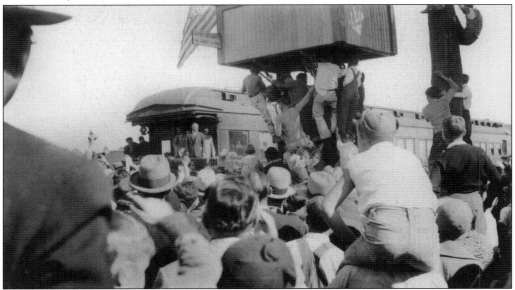

President Herbert Hoover, running for reelection, stopped at the Fullerton train depot in 1932. Hoover was in friendly company, winning in Orange County by better than a four-to-one margin. The depot was a popular spot for whistle-stop touring and such notables as saloon-smasher Carrie Nation (1902) and gubernatorial candidate Richard M. Nixon (1962) used the station for public appearances.

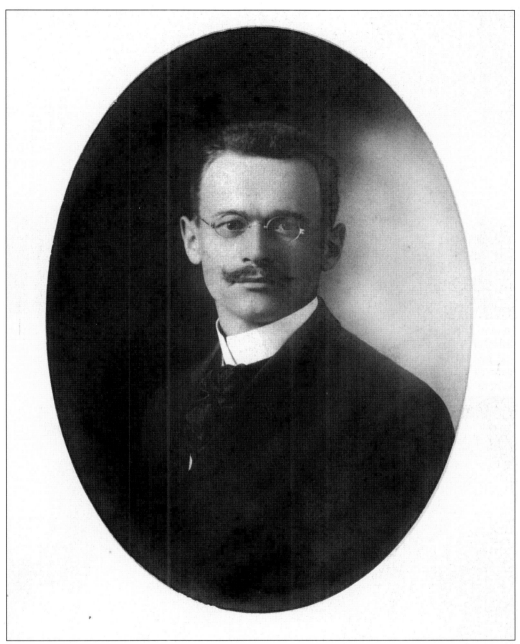

Born and college-educated in Bavaria, Johann George Seupelt (1877–1961) served as Fullerton's first park superintendent from 1918 to 1925, landscaping the grounds of Amerige and Hillcrest Parks and laying out the city's street trees. He was hired for government positions during World War I when anti-German sentiment was high and experienced discrimination while in Fullerton and in Spokane where he served as city forester from 1908 to 1915. He was one of the first individuals to receive an M.A. degree in landscape architecture, then a new field in America. (Photo courtesy of Northwest Museum of Arts & Culture, Eastern Washington State Historical Society, Spokane, Washington.)

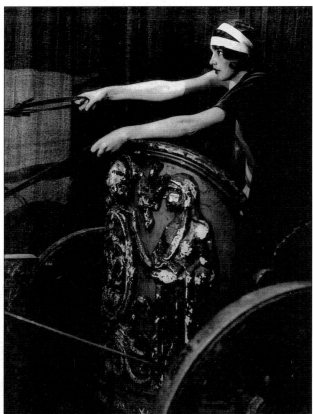

After graduating from Fullerton Union High School, philanthropist Doris Tennant Westcott enrolled at the University of Southern California where she was chosen in 1929 and 1930 as the first and second Helen of Troy, selected to represent the university at all social functions. During World War II she joined the WAVES as California's first woman in stripes. (Photo courtesy of USC Alumni Association.)

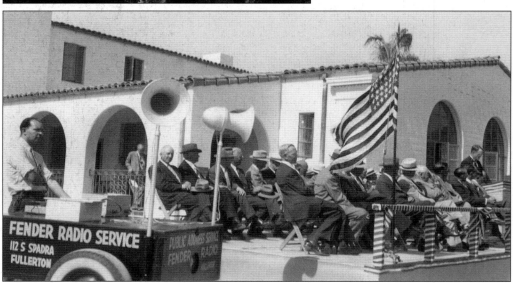

Clarence Leo Fender (1909–1991), the electric guitar pioneer whose Stratocasters have been played by such rock and roll legends as Buddy Holly, Eric Clapton, and Jimi Hendrix, began his career in public address systems. In this photo, Fender (left) is working at the cornerstone dedication of Fullerton's first city hall (now the police station) on June 28, 1941.

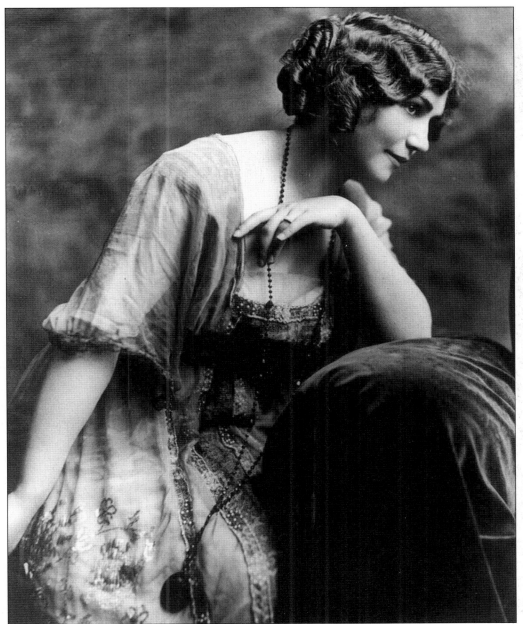

America's first woman filmmaker, Lois Weber (1881–1939) began her career as an actress, but in 1913 she began directing films and by 1916, working at Universal, she was one of the highest paid directors in the world. In 1917 she formed her own production company, and her career flourished until the early 1920s. Her films, which focused on such controversial and serious issues as birth control and abortion, brought her into constant conflict with distributors. Her second husband, Col. Herbert Gantz, built a large Spanish Colonial Revival home (El Dorado Ranch) on 100 acres for her. Although greatly "remuddled," the house now serves as the residence of the president of CSU Fullerton (225 West Union). (Photo courtesy of the Academy of Motion Picture Arts and Sciences.)

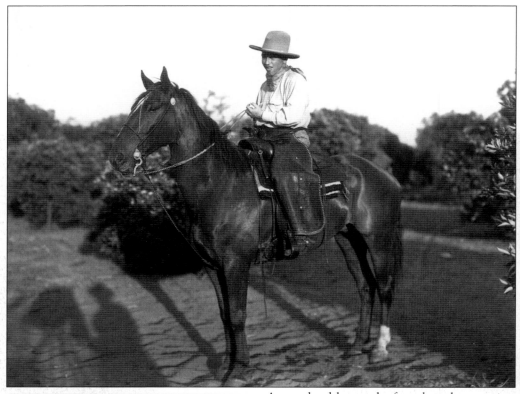

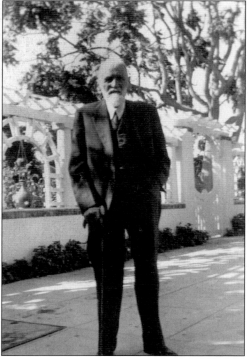

A superb athlete and a famed cowboy movie star, as well as an ordained minister, Fred Thomson (1890–1928) officiated at the marriage of Lois Weber and Herbert Gantz in 1926. The highest-paid Western star in Hollywood at one time, Thomson and his screenwriter wife, Frances Marion, were close friends of Weber, and the couple visited El Dorado Ranch where this photo was most likely taken.

A native of Germany, Frederick Stuelke (1845–1938) was the last surviving member of the Grand Army of the Republic (GAR) post in Fullerton. He enlisted in the Union Army in 1862 and took part in the siege of Vicksburg and Sherman's March to the Sea. After one battle, he was left on the field for dead, then captured by the Confederates and imprisoned in Andersonville, South Carolina.

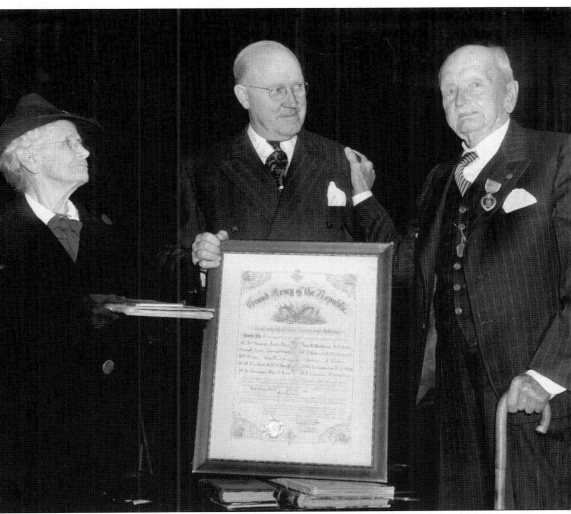

The last surviving member of the GAR in Orange County, William Burton Crandell (1850–1945) enlisted at the age of 12 (posing as a 20 year old) in the 52nd New York Infantry. After participating in major battles at Second Bull Run and Fredericksburg, he was seriously injured at Spottsylvania. At a Washington, D.C., hospital, President Lincoln visited the ward where Crandell was being treated, and after talking with the teenager, ordered his discharge for "youth and disability." Crandell is shown here (right) depositing the GAR papers now in the Fullerton Public Library.

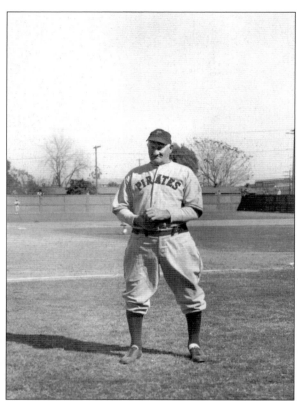

Coaching for the Pittsburgh Pirates, John Honus Wagner is shown in this photo standing in Amerige Park in 1938. Despite his long arms and bowed legs, Wagner was the greatest and fastest shortstop in baseball, earning the nickname "The Flying Dutchman." Wagner's baseball card is the most valuable card in the world.

On August 27, 1937, the first women's chapter of the Izaak Walton League of America was formed in the log cabin in Hillcrest Park. The idea of a place in conservation for women wasn't popular in the organization dedicated to hunting, fishing, and the outdoors. The group's first meeting featured little Laura Lee Bowie (right) as the performer.

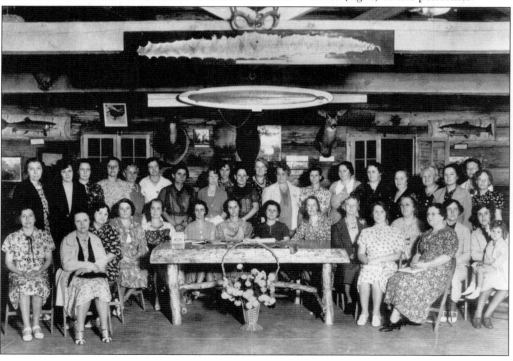

In the 1950s, Book Week at the Fullerton Public Library brought out many famous writers and entertainers. Here, Western writer Louis L'Amour (left) and political satirist Leonard Wibberly (center), author of *The Mouse That Roared*, sign books. Local poet Ethel Jacobson is on the right.

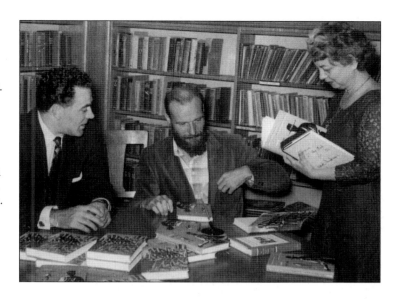

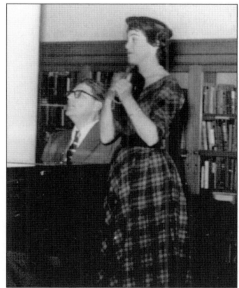

Composer Meredith Willson (*The Music Man*) and his wife, Rini, herself a star in the concert, radio, and opera business, belt out the "Iowa Fight Song." Rini is using her purse as a "tom-tom" or drum.

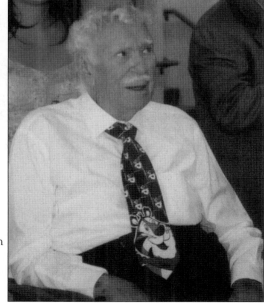

In this photo, the "grrrreat" Thurl Ravenstein celebrates his 90th birthday. Since 1952 Ravelstein has been the voice of Tony the Tiger in commercials for Kellogg's Frosted Flakes. (Photo courtesy of Barbara Giasone.)

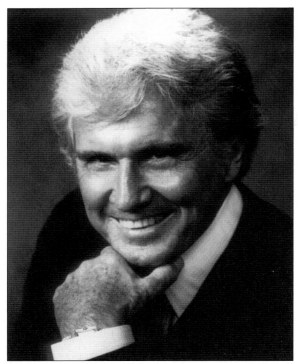

A star athlete and budding singer while at Fullerton Union High School, John Raitt went on to star on the Broadway stage and in theaters throughout America for 40 years. He attained Broadway stardom as Billy Bigelow, the carnival barker hero, in the original New York production of Rodgers and Hammerstein's *Carousel*. He is the father of blues singer Bonnie Raitt.

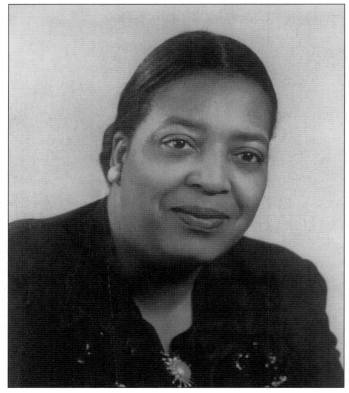

Ruby Goodwin (1903–1961) wrote her first book of poetry, *From My Kitchen Window*, in Fullerton, then went on to publish an acclaimed autobiography, *It's Good to Be Black*, and write a newspaper column on Black Hollywood. She was also publicist for actress Hattie McDaniel (*Gone with the Wind*) and gospel singer Ethel Waters, and in 1955, was named Mother of the Year for the State of California.

Two
STREETS AND AVENUES

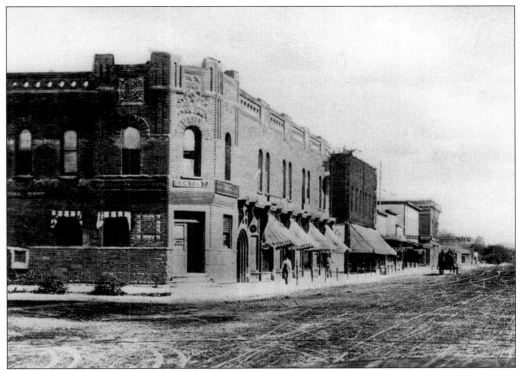

Looking north on Spadra Road (now Harbor Boulevard), this photograph showcases Fullerton's main thoroughfare in 1902. Fullerton's streets were not paved until 1914. Chadbourne Hall (left), with its brick façade, was one of the most impressive buildings of its day. It was used for meetings and social gatherings and also housed the city's first bank, the Fruit Growers Bank (1895), later the First National Bank.

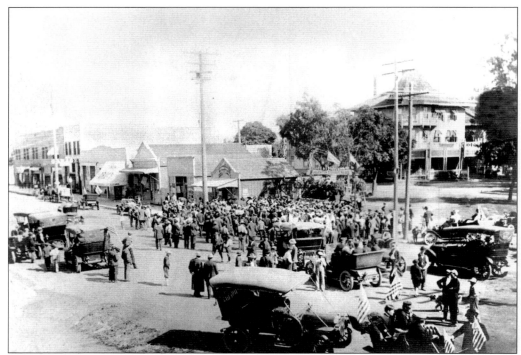

Looking northeast on Spadra Road, this photo shows Fullerton residents celebrating Founders' Day in May 1912. On the far right is the St. George Hotel, completed in February 1888. The small wooden building on the east side of the street is the Amerige Brothers Real Estate Office, the town's first commercial building.

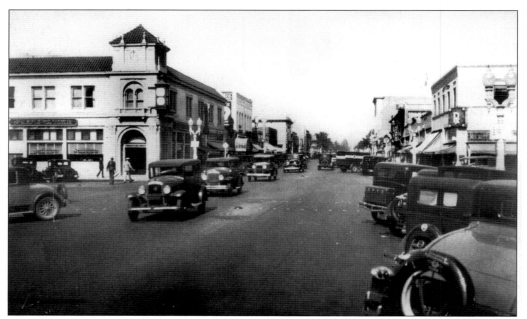

This photo shows Spadra Road looking north around 1925.

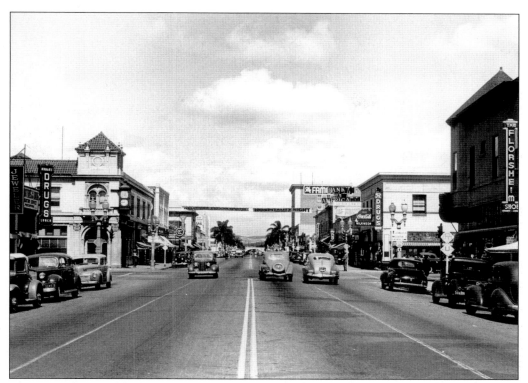

This is Spadra Road looking north in 1941. In the background is the Pacific Electric Railroad viaduct over Spadra. The sign for Highway 101, also called El Camino Real (the Royal Road), is on the east street sign. El Camino Real was pioneered by the Spaniards in the 1700s when they colonized California in the name of their king.

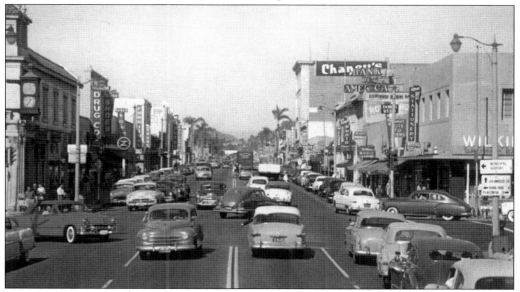

This postcard shows Spadra Road (renamed Harbor Boulevard in the 1960s) in 1951.

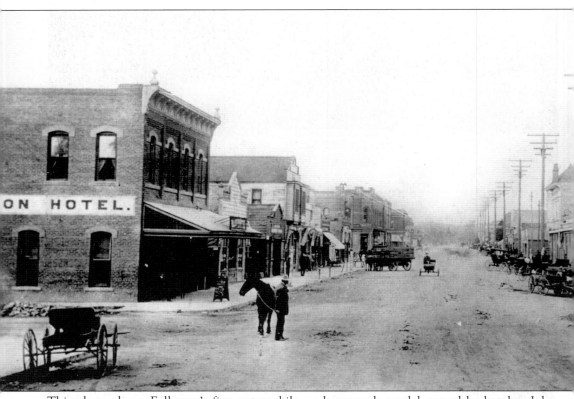

This photo shows Fullerton's first automobile—a homemade model owned by butcher John Hiltscher of Center Meats—putting down the middle of South Spadra Road in 1900.

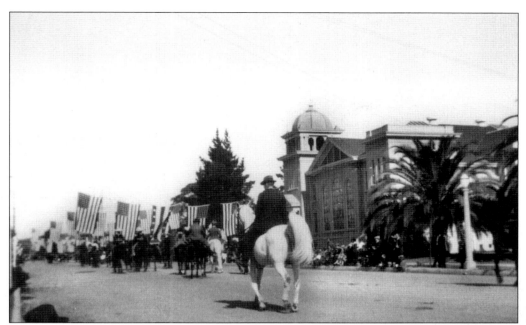

On November 11, 1922, four years after the close of World War I, Orange County residents staged the first armistice parade in Fullerton. This scene shows the parade on Pomona Avenue.

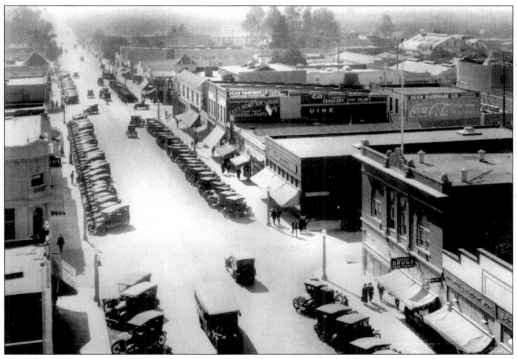

This 1925 photo, looking south toward Spadra Road, was taken from the top of the Chapman Building at 110 East Wilshire Avenue, then the tallest building in Orange County.

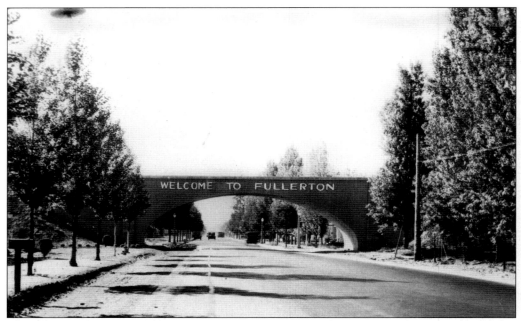

Constructed in 1917, the Pacific Electric Railroad viaduct over Spadra Road, shown here in 1927, was one of Fullerton's most recognizable landmarks. "Welcome to Fullerton" was written on the north side of the archway; "Fullerton—Come Again" on the south. When the landmark became a hazard to large trucks traveling down Spadra, it was razed in 1964.

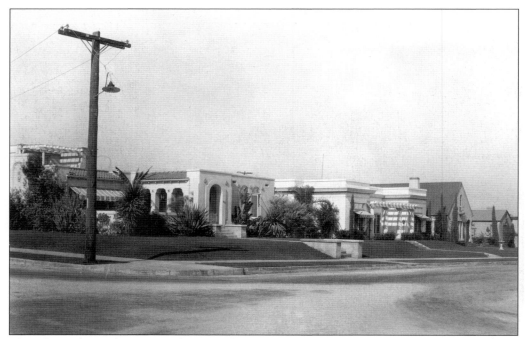

This photo shows the corner of Fern and Grandview in 1927 and is reflective of the middle-class residential neighborhoods that were springing up in Fullerton in the 1920s.

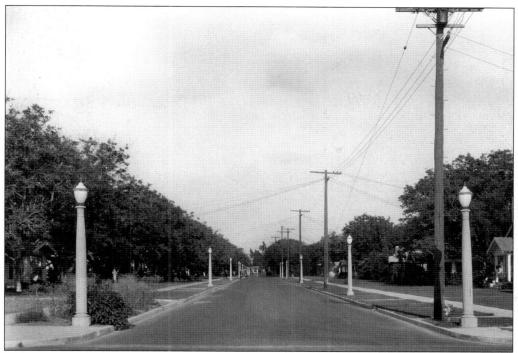

Taken from Ford Street in 1927, this photograph shows Malvern Avenue looking east toward Spadra Road.

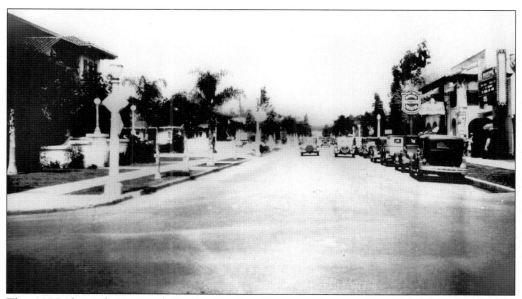

This 1927 photo shows North Spadra Road at Chapman Avenue. The Masonic Temple (now the Spring Field Banquet and Conference Center) is on the left. The Fox Fullerton Theatre, then known as the Universal Mission Theatre, is on the right. (Photo courtesy of First American Title.)

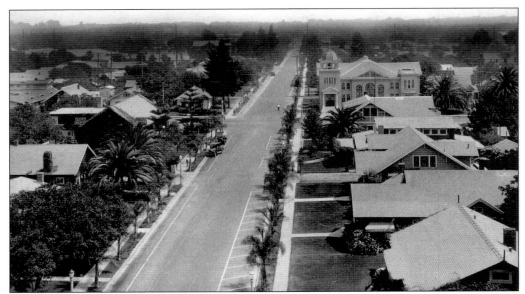

This 1920s postcard of East Wilshire Avenue was taken from the top of the Chapman Building. All of the dwellings in the 100 block were later demolished and replaced by commercial structures.

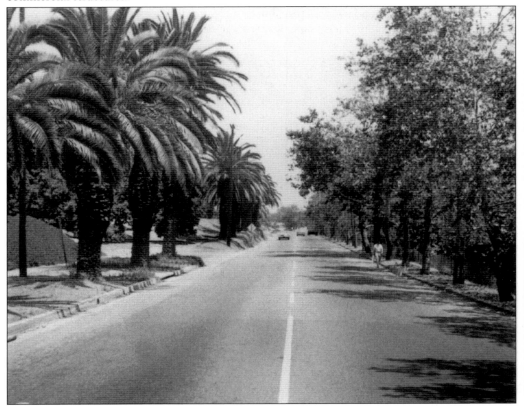

This is Chapman Avenue looking east from Euclid Avenue in July 1967.

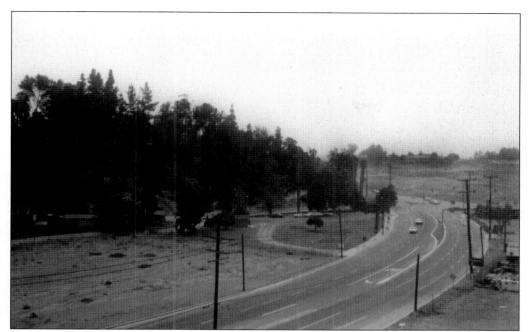

This is Brea Boulevard looking southwest to Harbor Boulevard in 1967. The tall trees on the left, planted in the 1920s and early 1930s, are part of Hillcrest Park. The vacant land on the top right is where the Ralphs Market complex now stands.

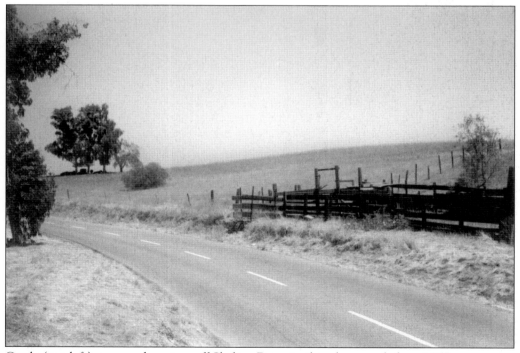

Cattle (top left) graze under a tree off Skyline Drive in this photograph from 1967.

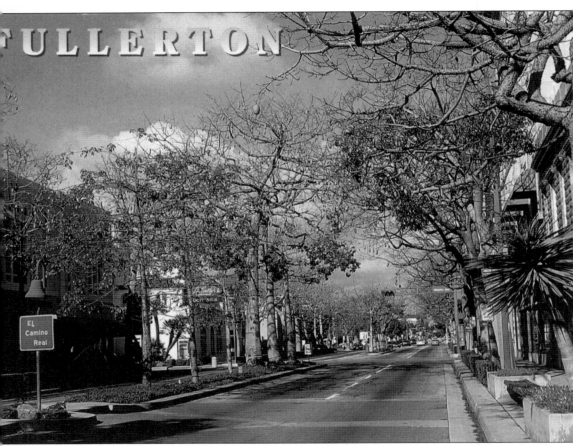

This is the 200 block of Harbor Boulevard around 2000. The El Camino Real bell, one of four originally in Fullerton, was the first bell placed in Orange County. The bells mark the El Camino Real road, which connected the chain of mission settlements established by the Spaniards when they colonized California. The road started as a foot trail connecting the missions between San Diego in the south and Sonoma nearly 600 miles north.

Three
BUSINESS AND INDUSTRY

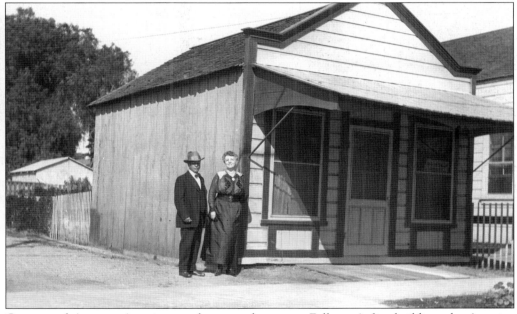

George and Annette Amerige stand next to downtown Fullerton's first building, the Amerige Brothers Real Estate Office, located at 109 South Spadra Road. For a time, the small office served as home for the Amerige brothers. Over the years, this simple frame building has served as a law office, barbershop, and tool shed. The restored structure is now in Amerige Park on Commonwealth Avenue.

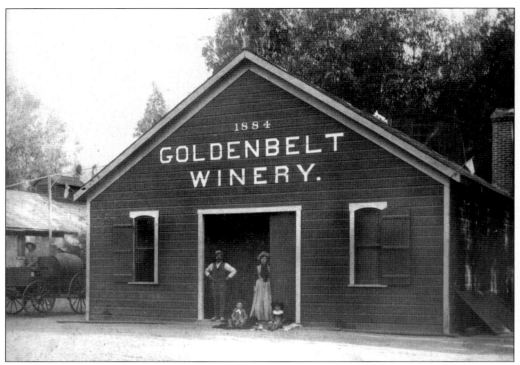

A number of wineries existed in the area, including the Goldenbelt Winery shown here, before Fullerton became a townsite. Fullerton's largest winery, located on East Chapman, was owned by William L. Hale. It was surrounded at the time by one of the largest vineyards in the state.

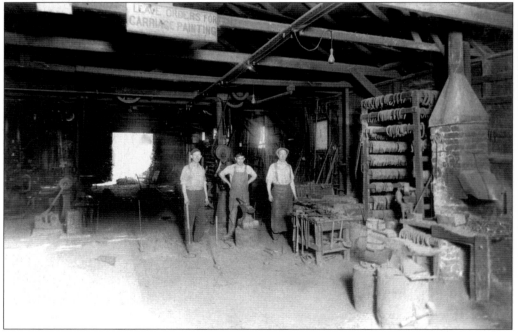

This photo shows the interior of Alex Henderson's blacksmith shop at 121 South Spadra Road.

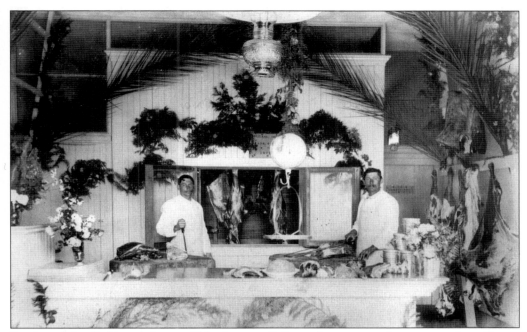

Brothers John (left) and August Hiltscher ran Fullerton's most popular meat market, Center Meats. The brothers' meat wagon also delivered goods to customers from their store on West Commonwealth. August served on the city council from 1908 to 1912 and again from 1913 to 1918. Hiltscher Park is named after him. John owned the first car in town.

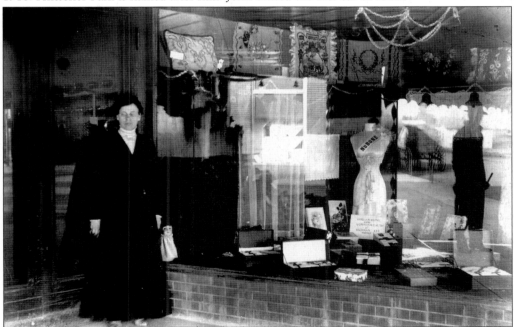

Company representative Mary E. Canfeld stands in front of the Fullerton headquarters for Nubone Corsets, a "strictly made-to-order" undergarment company at 204 North Spadra. A 1913 advertisement for the corset noted that it gave "a fine figure to stout ladies."

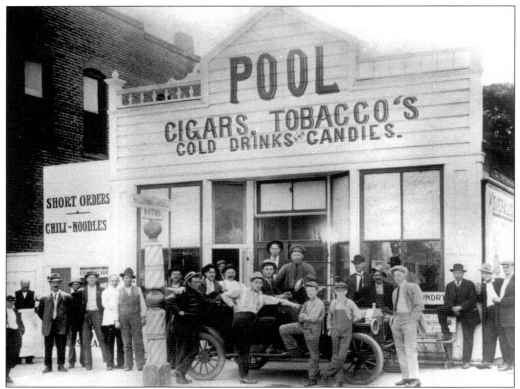

This late 1910s photograph shows the White Front Pool Room, located at 119 South Spadra Road.

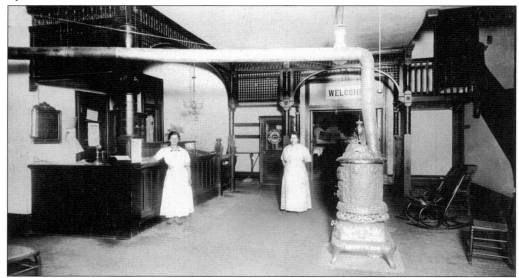

The lobby of the first-class Hotel Shay, formerly the St. George Hotel (1888), is shown here around 1915. Located one block from the Santa Fe Depot, the hotel was the first significant building in the newly established town. The hotel, which charged $2 a day, had 65 rooms with one bath on the second floor and one bath downstairs. It was razed in 1918.

This photograph shows the exterior of the economy Brandle Hotel at 100 South Spadra Road, named for owner Adam Brandle.

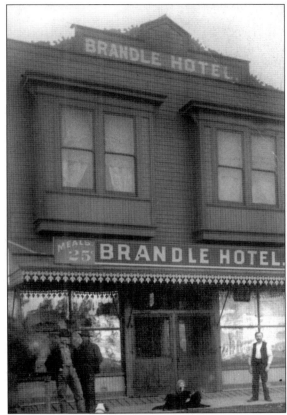

Pictured here are George and Emma Foster, proprietors of the local popcorn stand, stationed in front of the First National Bank at 122 North Spadra, the first bank building in Fullerton.

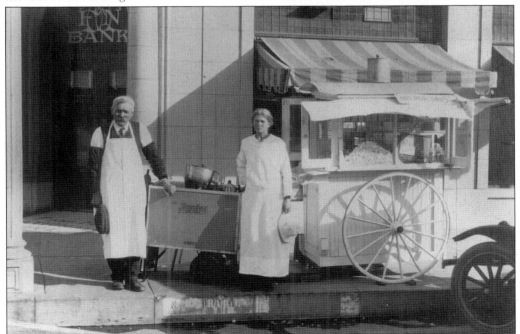

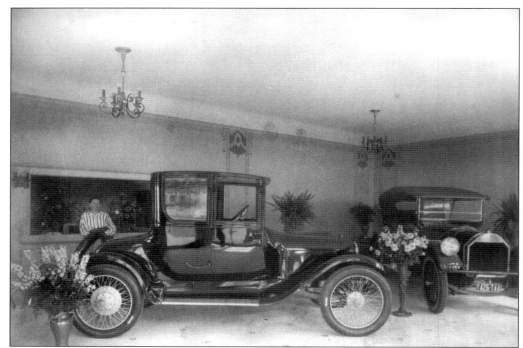

In 1919, Lillian Yaeger opened a Dodge Brothers dealership in Fullerton. One of the first people in Southern California to drive a car, Yaeger was one of Fullerton's first automobile dealers and Orange County's first service station operator. She was known for her spectacular swearing. Her residence at 108 West Brookdale Place (Le Potager) is said to be haunted by a ghost.

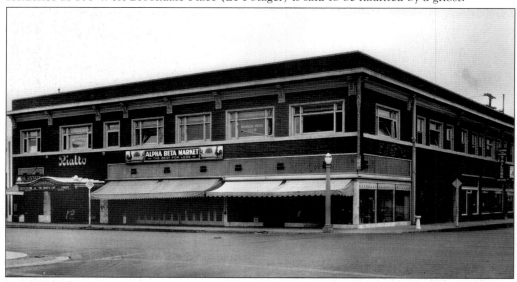

In 1928, Fullerton joined the growing ranks of Southern California towns that had an Alpha Beta Market. This photo shows market No. 19, located at 221 North Spadra. In 1915, company owner Albert C. Gerrard displayed his groceries alphabetically in Gerrard's Triangle Groceries (327 West Second, Pomona), to aid shoppers in finding goods, thus the name, "The Alpha Beta System." The company pioneered the concept of self-serve markets.

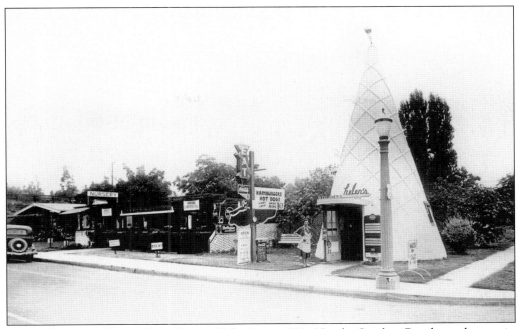

Originally named the Big Cone, Helen's at 900 North Spadra Road is shown in this photograph, taken around 1938. Owner Helen Eldred lived in a trailer behind the ice-cream shop.

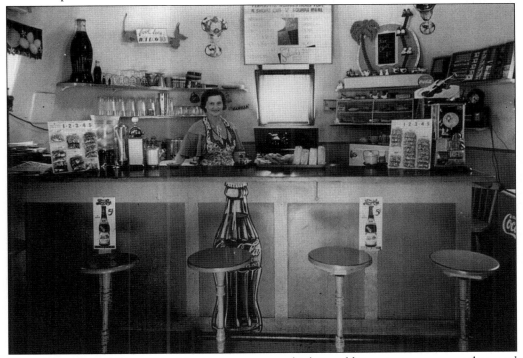

This photo shows Helen Eldred inside her eatery, which in addition to ice cream, cokes, and hamburgers, sold a foot-long hot dog for 10¢.

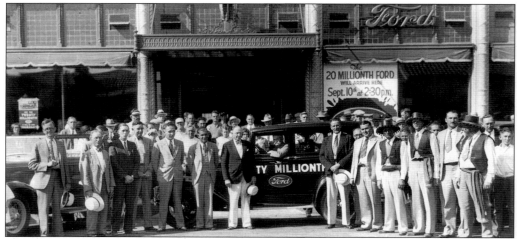

On September 10, 1931, Ford Motor Company representatives came to town to celebrate the arrival of the 20-millionth Ford produced and sold. The celebration took place at the McCoy and Mills Ford dealership at 125 West Commonwealth Avenue. Mayor William L. Hale is seated in the car. The dealership was destroyed by fire in 1950, prompting McCoy and Mills to move to a new facility that continues to operate today.

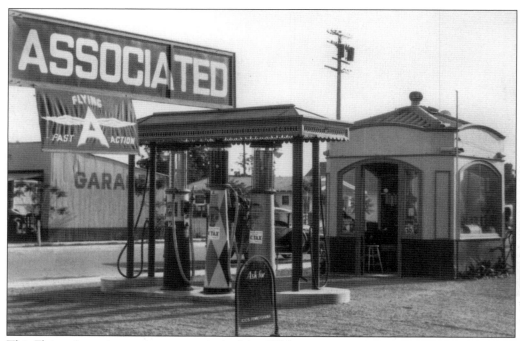

This Flying A service station was typical of the 1920s.

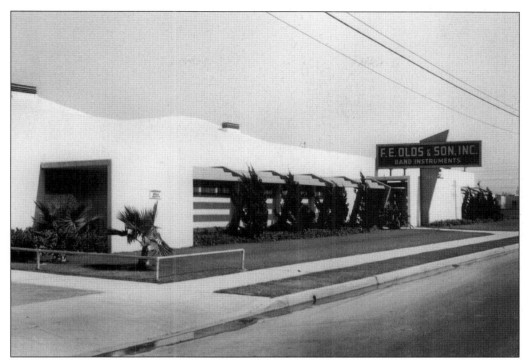

Founded by Frank E. Olds and his son Reginald, the F.E. Olds & Son Company moved to 350 North Raymond in Fullerton in 1954. By the time the company closed its doors in 1978, it had manufactured hundreds of thousands of metal wind instruments that were used throughout the world. Today the instruments are highly valued by collectors.

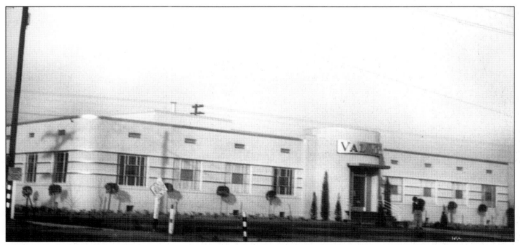

In 1932, industrialist Norton Simon, only 23, purchased Val-Vita Food Products Inc., a citrus juice plant, and joined it with Hunt Foods Inc., and then went on to turn the business into the multinational Hunt-Wesson, Inc. This company office building at 1731 West Commonwealth is the only Streamline Moderne commercial building in Fullerton.

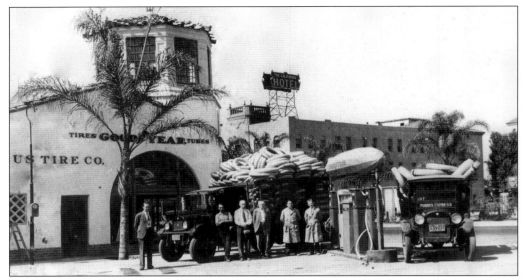

The Citrus Tire Company was located on the southwest corner of Whiting and Spadra. In the background of this photo is the California Hotel (Villa del Sol) and on the right is the Tom Thumb Miniature Golf Course. The wishing well from the golf course is now in the backyard of the Foster House.

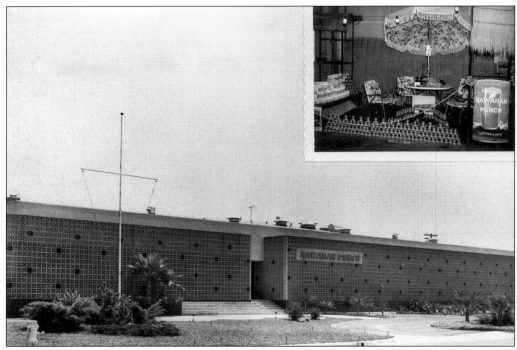

In 1931, food chemist A.W. Leo opened a two-man plant, the Citrus Products Company at 120 West Amerige, and began producing Hawaiian Punch, a then exotic drink that combined pineapple, guava, papaya, and passion fruit. By 1959, the company was making millions of dollars annually and moved into new headquarters at 360 South Acacia, expanding its product line to include Hawaiian Nectar, Lime Rickey, and Hula Highball.

Four
PARKS, RECREATION, AND LEISURE

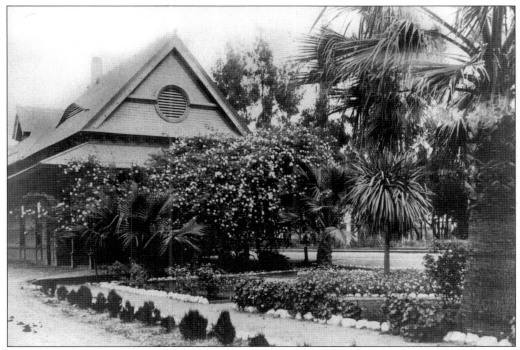

In October 1904 Fullerton city trustees contacted the Santa Fe Railroad about establishing the city's first park. The railroad furnished the land and gardener and Fullerton the plant materials, and Santa Fe Park was born. The Santa Fe Depot, shown on the left, was built in 1888 and demolished in 1929 to make way for the Spanish Colonial Revival–Santa Fe/Amtrak Depot.

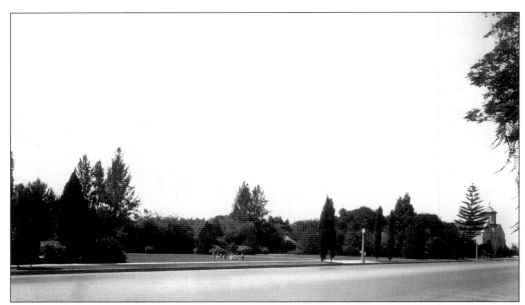

When Fullerton High School burned down on March 18, 1910, a movement began to obtain the site for a park, and in 1913, Commonwealth (later Amerige) Park, shown here in 1920, was established as Fullerton's first city-owned park. St. Mary's Roman Catholic Church (1912), shown on the right, was destroyed by a fire in 1968 and replaced by a more modern-looking building.

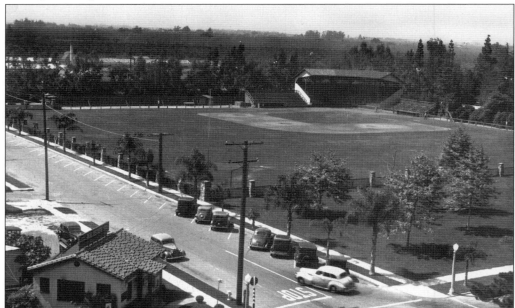

Additional acreage was added to Amerige Park, and this dirt field served as a ball field for countless players. In 1934, Fullerton used WPA funds to greatly improve the field, which soon became a training site for farm and semi-professional baseball teams and exhibition games that featured such Hall of Famers as Joe DiMaggio, Satchel Paige, and Bob Lemon. This 1940s photo was taken from the Fullerton City Hall (1942) tower.

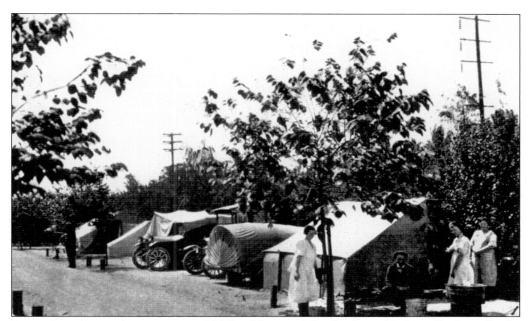

Located on the southwest corner of Valley View and Spadra (now Harbour Boulevard), the Fullerton Municipal Auto Camp was the first area of Hillcrest Park to be developed. The auto camp, which had water, gas, and electric lights, opened in October 1920. The camp was replaced in 1936 by a fountain area and lawn built by Depression-era workers.

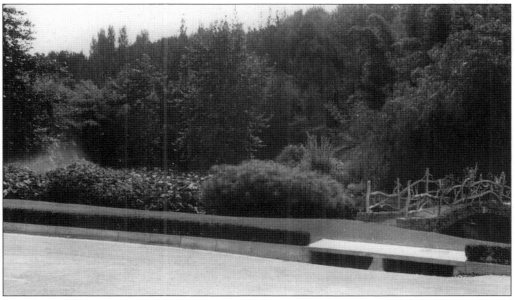

In 1922, a lily pond, formal flower garden, and cactus garden were added to the northwest corner of Hillcrest Park off Brea Boulevard. The bridge on the right, added in 1934, and other rockwork built around the parkland during the Depression were a contributing factor when Hillcrest Park was placed on the National Register of Historic Places in 2004.

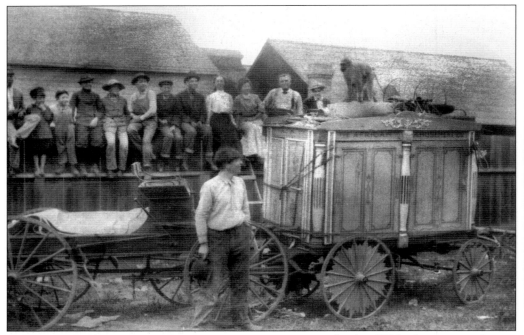

In this 1890s photo, a monkey performs for local residents as part of the African Amusement Company's traveling show.

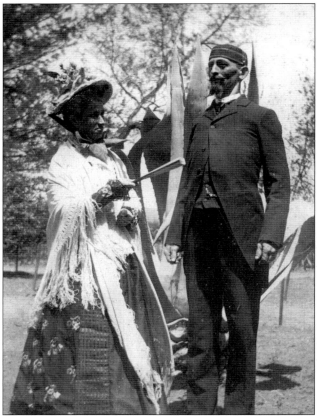

Town pioneer Otto des Granges and his daughter-in-law Jennie show off their fancy attire for a costume party on April 23, 1899. Now razed, the des Granges family home at 2000 East Wilshire was once the oldest in Fullerton.

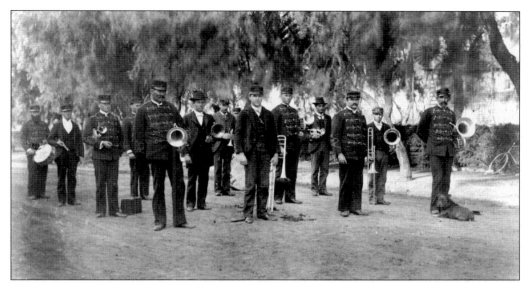

Active from 1892 to 1899, the Fullerton Band entertained at parades, political rallies, serenades, and dances, and sponsored an annual New Year's Eve masquerade ball at Chadbourne Hall that became a tradition in Orange County. The community placed a high value on music and had two halls, Chadbourne Hall and McDermot's Hall, where artistic programs as well as large political rallies were held.

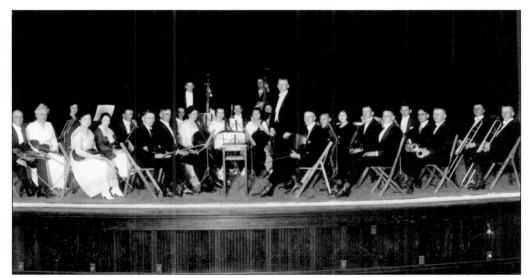

This photo shows the Orange County Orchestra performing in the high school auditorium in 1921. Conductor Harold Walberg (standing in the center) arrived in Fullerton in 1919 and quickly became the head of the music departments for Fullerton Union High School and Fullerton College.

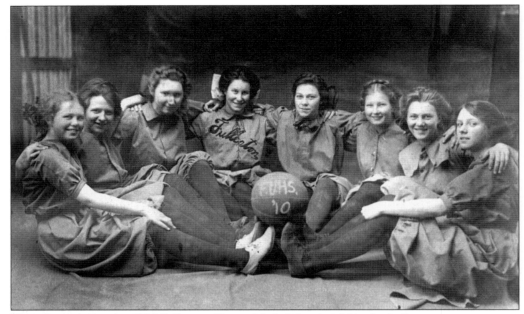

This photo shows the 1910 Fullerton Union High School girls' basketball team.

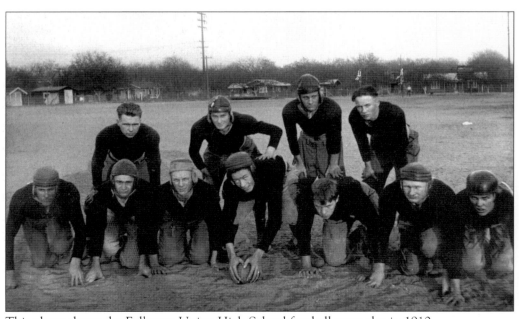

This photo shows the Fullerton Union High School football team also in 1910.

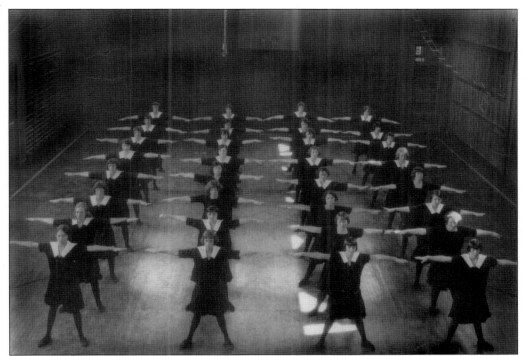

Taken in the 1920s, this photo shows the Fullerton Union High School girls' gym class in perfect formation.

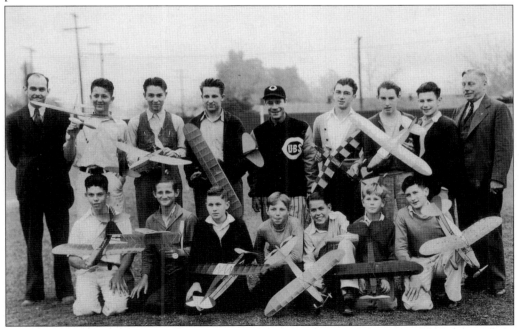

Famous actor and comedian Joe E. Brown (center) poses with members of the Fullerton Hawks Model Aircraft Club in 1935. Brown (*Some Like It Hot*, *Showboat*), known for his rubbery face, wide mouth, and loud voice, was in town filming *Alibi Ike* in Amerige Park.

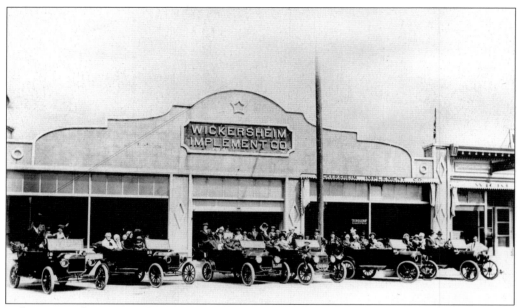

Fullerton residents immediately embraced the automobile and began organizing community events around this new technology. In this photo from the late 1910s, residents are lined up in front of the Wickersheim Implement Company at 117–125 West Commonwealth for an automobile trip.

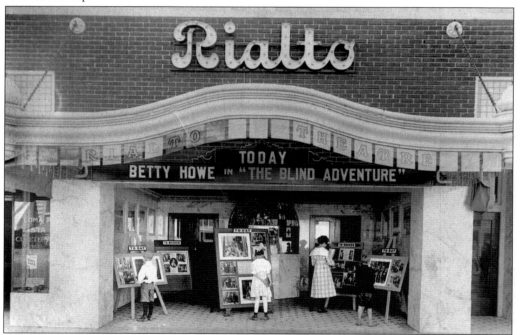

The third of five theaters in Fullerton, the Rialto (1917–1927) at 219 North Spadra Road showed the most current silent films of the day. In 1930, the theater was turned into the First National Trust Bank and its façade was redesigned into a Zigzag Moderne style by the notable architectural firm of Walker and Eisen. It has remained unaltered since then.

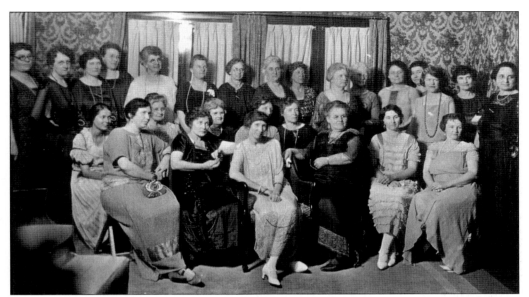

Organized March 9, 1909, the PEO Sisterhood, Chapter Y, shown here in the 1920s, met in the homes of members on alternate Thursdays. Fullertonians have always been joiners, and dozens of fraternal, patriotic, and community organizations were formed even before the city incorporated in 1904.

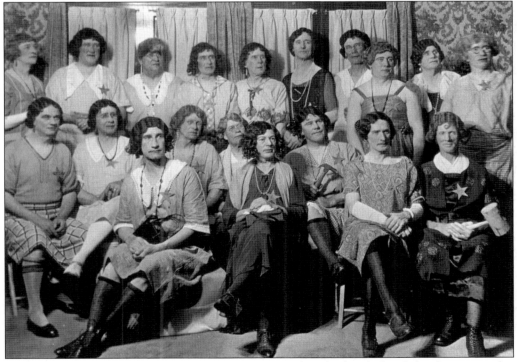

While members of the PEO Sisterhood were meeting, their husbands decided to have some fun of their own.

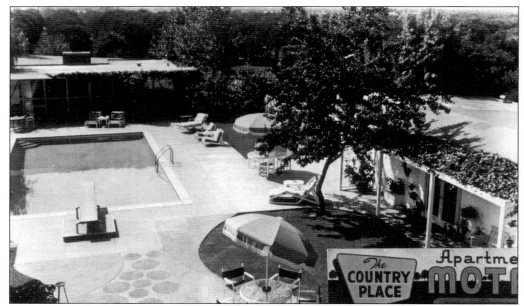

Located at 9862 Orangethorpe, the County Place Motel was one of a number of motels that sprang up in the 1950s and 1960s to accommodate increased tourist traffic to the area. The motel was advertised as being "between Disneyland and Knott's Berry Farm."

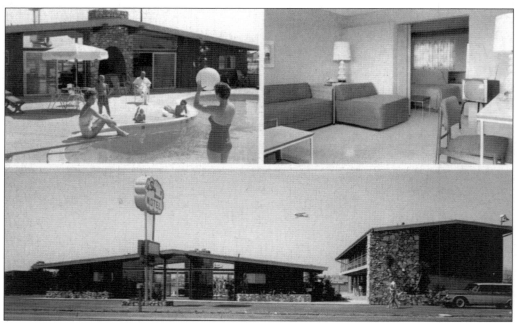

Adjacent to the Fullerton Airport, the Sky Haven Motel at 4251 West Commonwealth was advertised as a "drive in or fly in" accommodation ("Park your plane and step in—on the airport"). Opened in 1962, the motel featured such luxury items as a heated pool, free television, and room phones.

Five

HOUSES, RANCHES, AND APARTMENTS

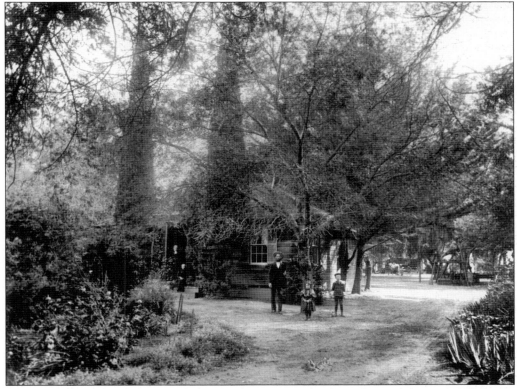

Taken in the 1890s, this photo shows the des Granges family in front of their ranch home at 2000 East Wilshire, once known as the oldest in Fullerton. The family members from left to right are Josephine, Jennie, Otto, Marie, and Paul. A native of Prussia, Germany, Otto came to the area in 1893 and purchased 80 acres east of Acacia. The southwest corner of the property, originally devoted to walnut and orange production, is now part of Ladera Vista Junior High.

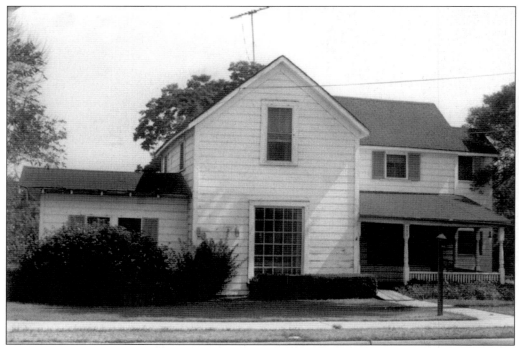

Very typical of the period, this wood-framed grovehouse is now the oldest existing home in Fullerton. Originally built by John Kerr in 1882, this Colonial Revival at 771 West Orangethorpe first stood in the midst of a vineyard. It was farmed until 1952, and other crops included apricots, plums, walnuts, and oranges.

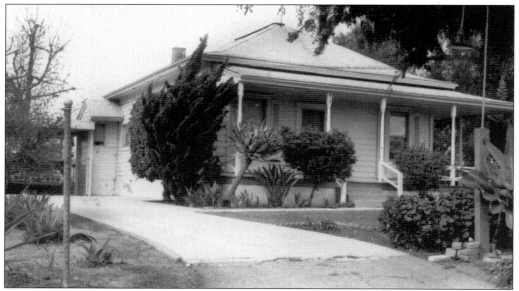

The Noutary House at 213 Claire is one of the very few in Fullerton that shows how the area must have looked originally. Constructed in 1901, the Colonial Revival farmhouse was the only building in this part of town until the 1930s, when the Northgate Heights area was subdivided for residential development.

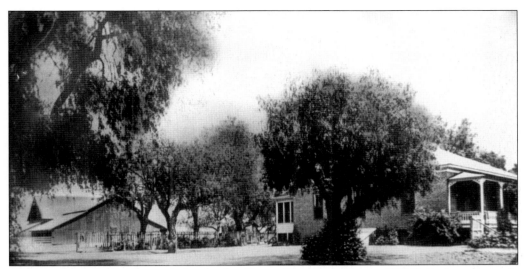

Constructed with locally-made brick, the Henry Hetebrink House (1886) is the only early residence of this type of construction still remaining in Fullerton. Now known as the Titan House, it sits on the CSU Fullerton campus. The Hetebrink family originally used the 160-acre property to operate one of the few dairy farms in the area.

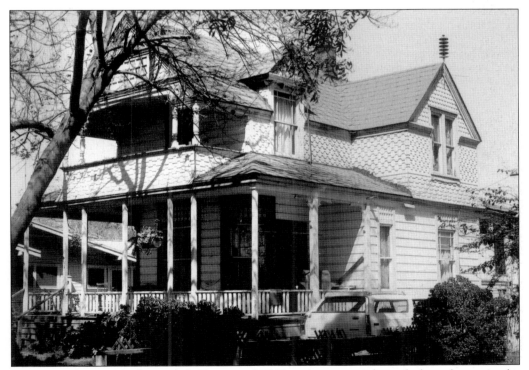

Constructed in 1895, the Cusick House at 315 East Amerige is the only large house in the Queen Anne style intact in Fullerton. Known for its exuberance, the Queen Anne style was invented in England about 1860 and copied by American architects from 1880 to 1900. The house was saved from a proposed demolition and lovingly restored in 1993.

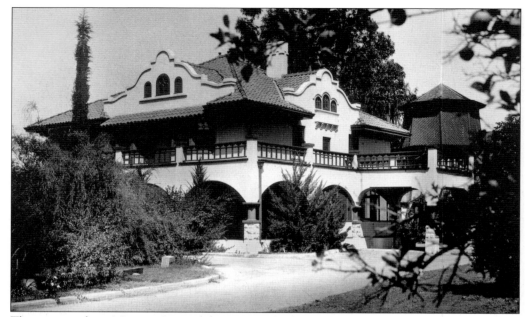

This outstanding Mission Revival home was built for Mayor William L. Hale in 1908. Originally situated on a 28-acre ranch among walnut and orange groves, the house was considered one of the showplaces in Orange County in the early 1900s. It was converted into the Montessori Child Development Center (2025 East Chapman) in the 1970s.

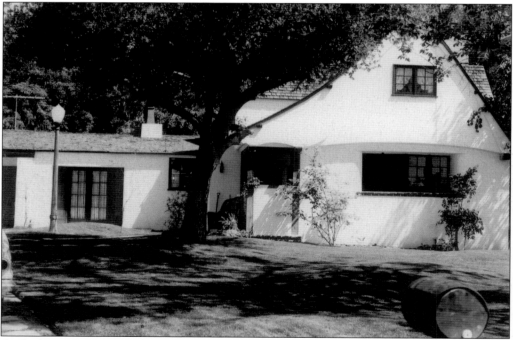

An Irish country manor, the Starbuck House at 834 North Woods was constructed in 1927 for Raymond Starbuck, the son of town pioneer William Starbuck, owner of the city's first drugstore, the Gem Pharmacy.

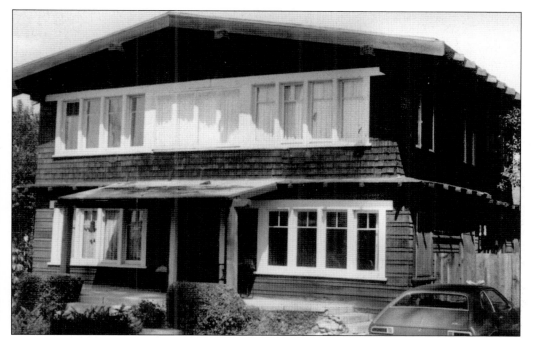

Located at 419 West Commonwealth, the Gallemore House, constructed in 1913, is an exceptionally fine example of the Shingle style. Owner J.R. Gallemore was the president of the Fullerton News Publishing Company until 1922.

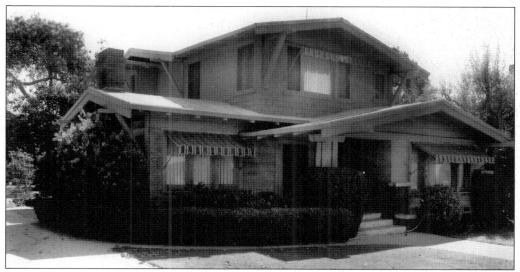

This impressive Craftsman-style bungalow at 604 North Harbor was built in 1915 for Edward K. Benchley, a prominent businessman and Fullerton's second mayor. Along with Charles C. Chapman, Benchley was instrumental in initiating and promoting the orange packing industry. The home was designed by Benchley's son Frank the architect of several notable buildings in Fullerton and Anaheim.

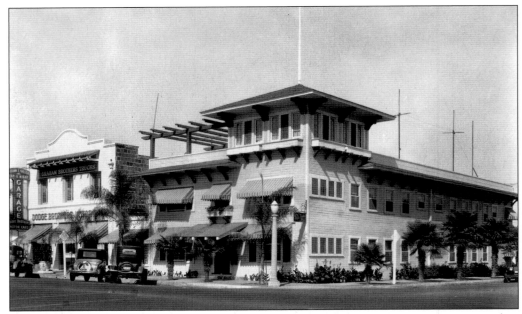

One of Fullerton's first apartment complexes, the Marwood Apartments were constructed in 1913 on North Spadra (now Harbor) by Dr. William Wickett, the son-in-law of Charles C. Chapman, Fullerton's first mayor. The building, located on the northeast corner of Whiting and Harbor, was demolished in 1980. Lillian Yaeger's Dodge Brothers dealership and filling station (the first in the county) are on the left.

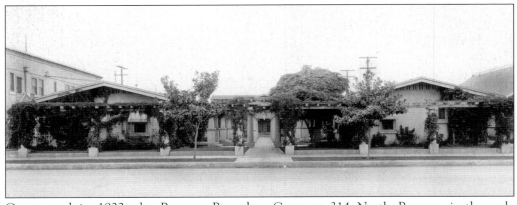

Constructed in 1922, the Pomona Bungalow Court at 314 North Pomona is the only Craftsman-style court in Fullerton. The 10-unit complex was designed by notable local architect Frank Benchley, who also designed the California Hotel (Villa del Sol), the Farmers and Merchants Bank, the Muckenthaler Cultural Center, and the former Masonic Temple, now the Spring Field Banquet and Conference Center.

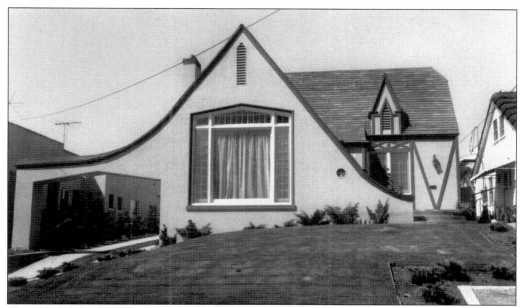

This picturesque English cottage-style home at 701 North Richman was built as a model home in 1927 by the chamber of commerce to promote the sale of homes in Fullerton. Promotional literature proclaimed that the home was "Built up to the standard . . . not down to a price." Despite its status as a model home, no others like it were ever built in Fullerton.

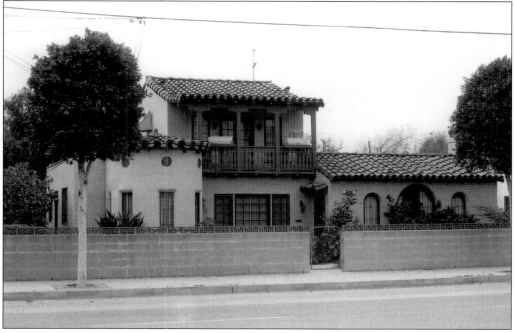

Constructed by Albert Foster, a prominent cement and gravel contractor, the Foster House at 524 East Commonwealth is an innovative Spanish Colonial Revival dwelling that also has a three-unit apartment in the rear. The house's front window—a stained-glass, bronco-riding roper—has been a conversation piece for passersby since the residence went up in 1929.

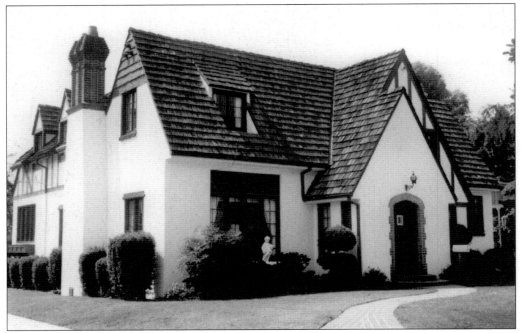

The Lamhofer House at 600 West Valley View Drive is one of the finest examples of English Tudor Revival architecture in Fullerton. Norton Simon, president of Hunt-Wesson, Inc., lived here between 1936 and 1938.

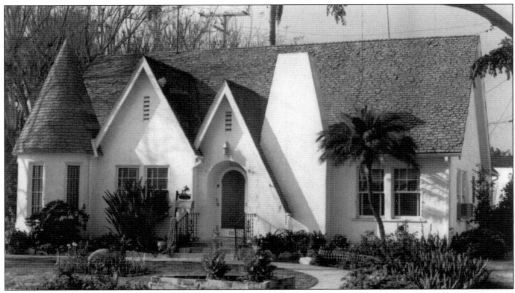

Locally referred to as "the castle," the Conley House at 1101 East Whiting is part of a small tract of Storybook-style homes built by E.S. Gregory in the late 1920s along the north side of Whiting Avenue. This style, which copies older styles, is known by names such as the Cottage style, Cinderella style, or Hansel and Gretel style.

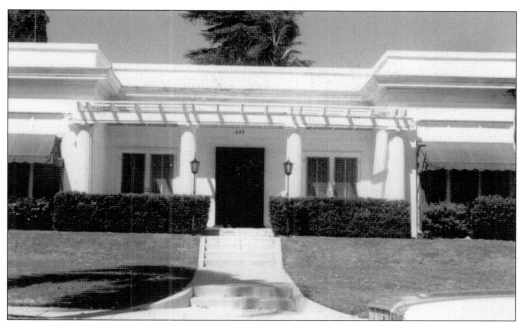

Constructed for Arthur Kelley in 1923, this house at 539 West Fern Drive was one of the earliest in the Golden Hills tract. An interpretation of a Roman villa, the residence is a unique example of the Neoclassical Revival style in Fullerton.

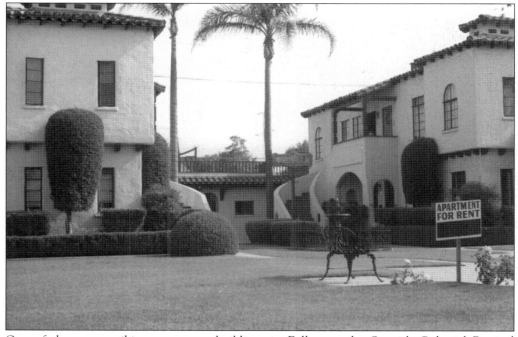

One of the most striking apartment buildings in Fullerton, the Spanish Colonial Revival Dewella Apartments at 232–236 East Wilshire were built for $11,000 in 1929.

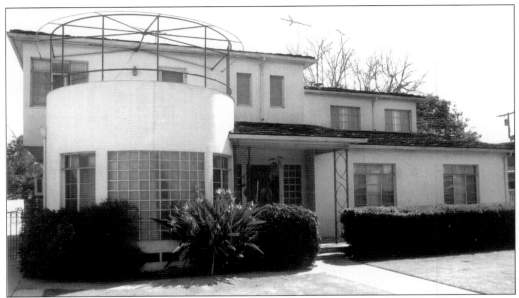

Town founder George Amerige constructed this house at 616 North Harbor in 1938. Amerige moved here after living in a second-floor apartment above the Amerige block at 109–123 East Commonwealth, a commercial structure built in 1920. The house is a unique combination of the Cottage style and Streamline Moderne.

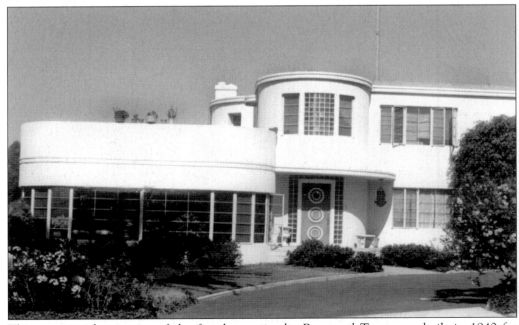

This two-story home, one of the first homes in the Raymond Tract, was built in 1940 for Richard Gamble, co-owner of the Proctor and Gamble Company, for $16,000. This unique dwelling, located at 1313 North Raymond, is the only Streamline Moderne home in Fullerton.

Six

OIL, AGRICULTURE, AND TRANSPORTATION

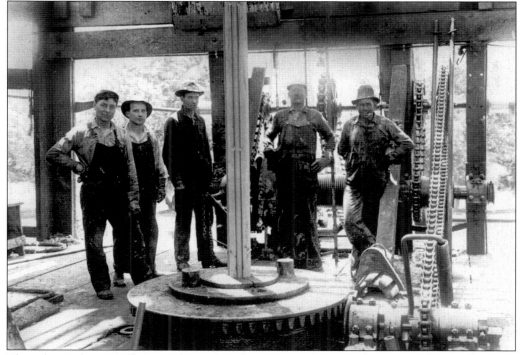

This photo shows Fullerton's first oil well around 1890. Revenues from the "black gold" sustained Fullerton's government for the next 50 years.

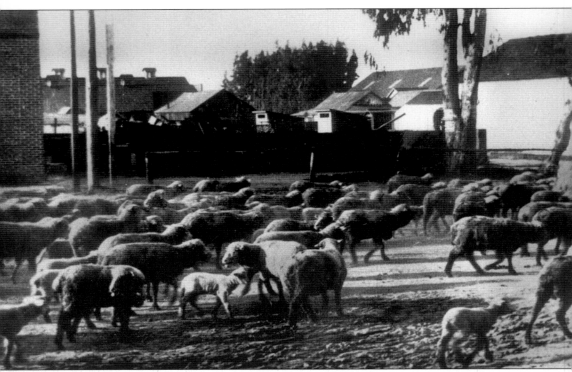

Cotton shortages caused by the Civil War and the reconstruction period prompted Domingo Bastanchury to purchase land in the mid-1860s and develop the largest herd of sheep in the area. In this 1890s photo, Bastanchury sheep are being herded through downtown Fullerton toward the train station. The sheep ranch in northern Fullerton was later converted to what was called the largest orange grove in the world.

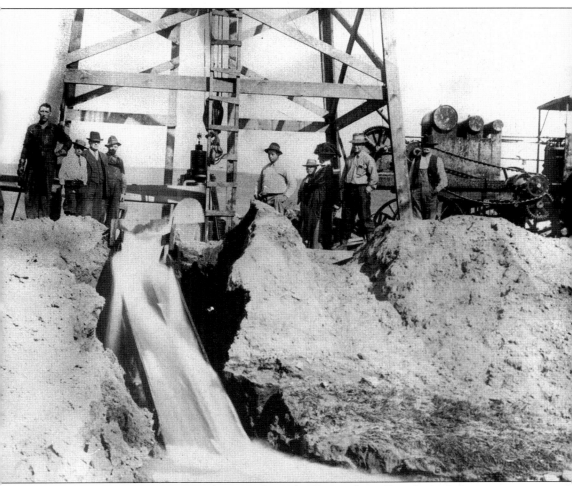

In 1914 great artisan springs were discovered on the Bastanchury Ranch, and the water is still distributed by the Bastanchury Water Company. Domingo Bastanchury could not read or write and relied on this wife, Maria (center in black), to deal with recordkeeping and formal business dealings.

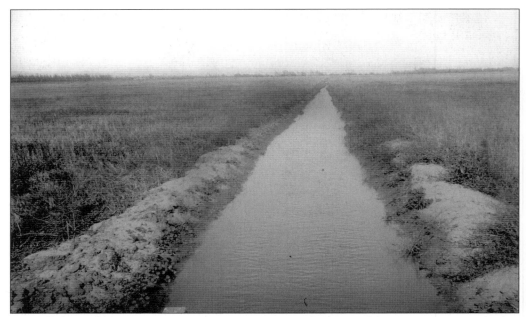

For Fullerton's first water system, George Amerige used Chinese laborers to excavate ditches like the one shown here in 1887 down what is now Harbor Boulevard.

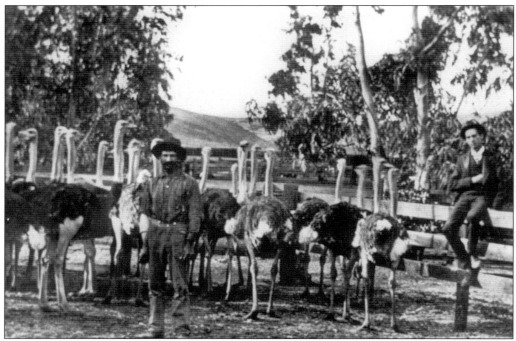

In the 1880s, the Fullerton Ostrich Farm belonging to Edward Atherton, located at the northeast corner of Dorothy and Acacia, became a prime tourist attraction.

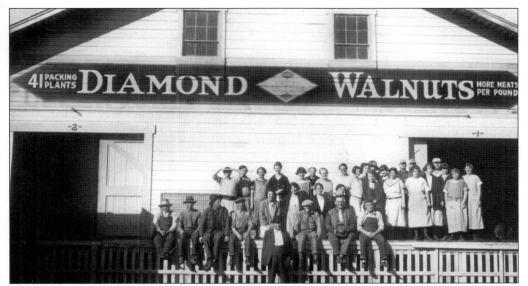

Around 1910 citrus began to dominate agricultural production, but before that, walnuts were the largest crop produced in Fullerton. The Fullerton Diamond Walnuts packinghouse, shown here in 1924, was one of many that packed nuts for shipping. Diamond Walnuts, a company founded by farm families from California, was launched in 1912.

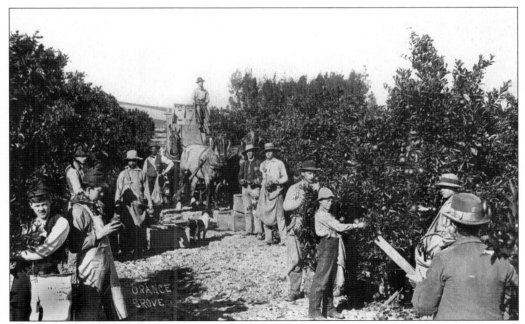

In this photograph from 1894, orange pickers are shown working on the William F. Botsford Ranch. Orange plantings began extensively in Fullerton in the 1880s and citrus quickly became the primary crop produced.

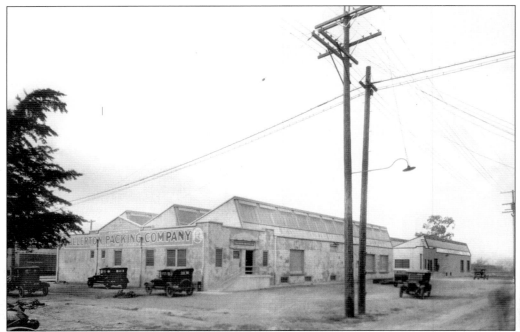

By 1899 Fullerton had become the principal shipping point south of Los Angeles, and by 1920 over two million boxes of oranges alone were being shipped annually. To keep up with the demand, dozens of packinghouses, including the Fullerton Packing Company (1923) at 114 West Walnut, sprang up around the train station. The citrus-railroad link became the foundation of Fullerton's economy.

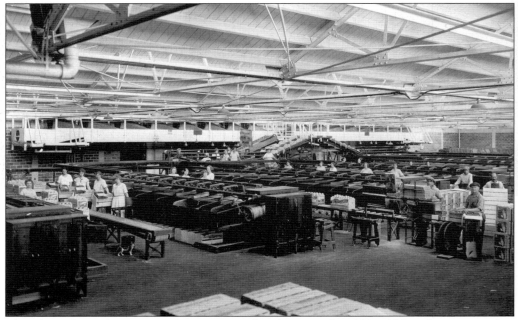

This photo shows the interior of an orange packinghouse in the 1920s. Although men were first employed in the packing plants, women workers gradually replaced them.

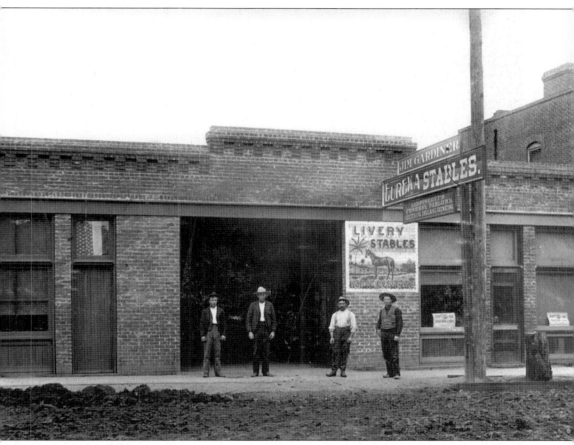

Pioneer James Gardiner's Eureka Stables (1897), located in the 100 block of West Commonwealth, served as Fullerton's first form of transportation. The sign indicates that Lippincott's Funeral Parlors ("Undertaking, Embalming, Cremating") is the building on the right.

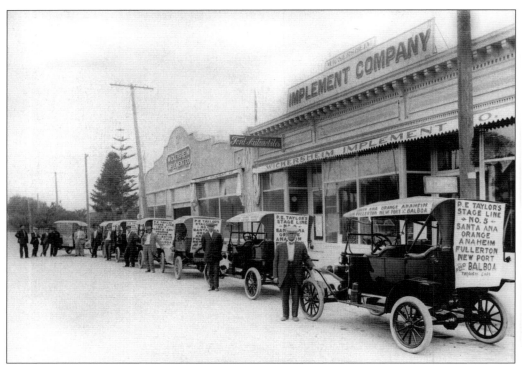

Taken in the 1920s, this photo shows vehicles from P.E. Taylor's Stage Line lined up to take passengers on six different automobile routes throughout Southern California.

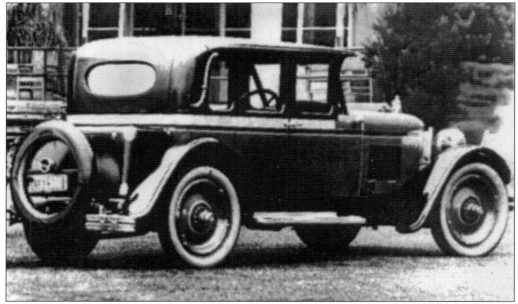

In 1925, after eight years of preparation and experiment, the Balboa Motor Company was launched with the plan to manufacture 1000 sedans and sports broughams at a cost of $2,900 each. Although the touring car's engine was progressive for the time, only two cars and one chassis were ever completed. The company quickly died amidst stock promotion fraud charges.

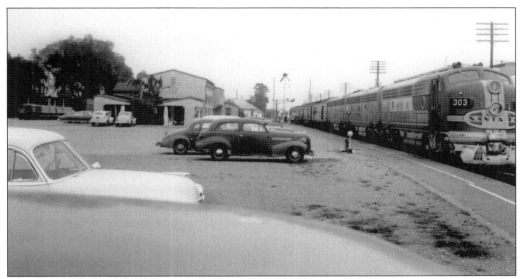

This photo shows the Fullerton train station in the late 1940s. In the rear is the second Santa Fe Depot (1930). At the time, packinghouses still lined the train track.

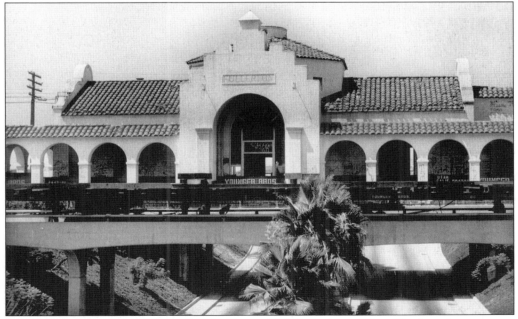

In 1980, the abandoned Union Pacific Depot (1923), built on West Truslow Avenue, was moved to its current location at the new Transportation Center. The depot, which now houses the Old Spaghetti Factory restaurant, is one of only five Mission Revival–style buildings remaining in Fullerton.

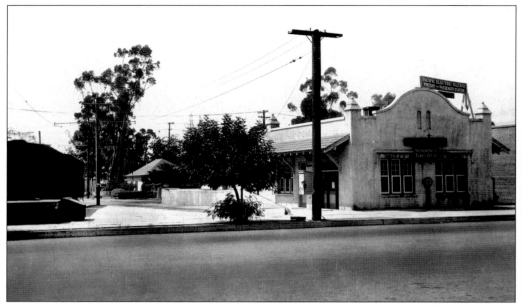

The Pacific Electric Railway came to Fullerton in 1917 as an extension from the La Habra line. The depot (now Spadra Restaurant) at 136 East Commonwealth was constructed in 1918 at a cost of $10,000.

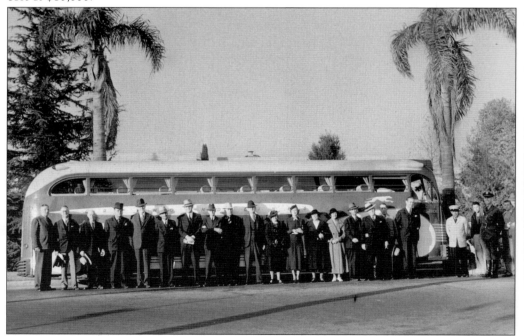

In 1938, the PE Depot began a new life as the Pacific Greyhound Lines bus depot, which lasted until 1976. Pacific Greyhound had established the first continental bus system in the United States in 1928. In this photo, Mayor Harry Maxwell (sixth from left) stands with Fullerton's first bus passengers, who are preparing to board "Super Coach" model 743, the first bus to introduce air conditioning and diesel fuel.

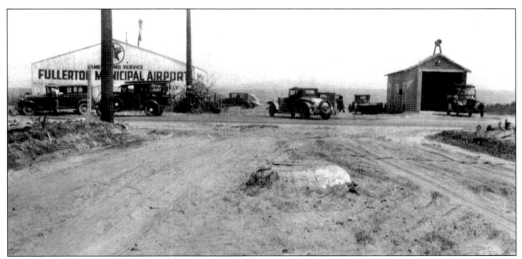

In 1927, pioneer aviators William and Richard Dowling convinced the city to establish an airfield on land previously used as a hog farm, then a sewer operation. The 86-acre Fullerton Municipal Airport, shown here in the early 1930s, is the oldest and largest general aviation airfield still in its original location in Orange County. It has an aircraft capacity of 600 planes.

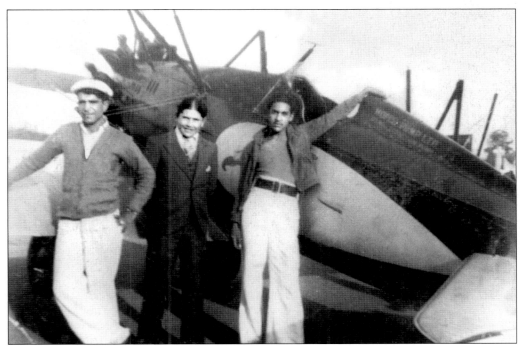

Paul Guzman (center) and two friends are shown at the Fullerton Municipal Airport around 1933. (Photo courtesy of Shades of L.A. Archives, Los Angeles Public Library.)

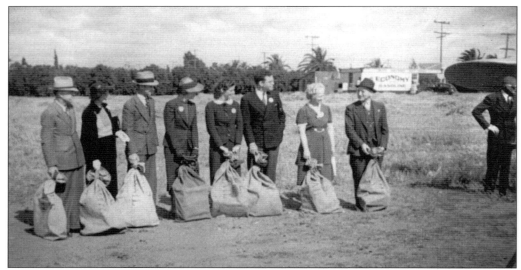

At 3:20 p.m. on May 19, 1938, the first airmail flight from the community was made from the Fullerton Municipal Airport. Eight north Orange County postmasters brought 50 pounds of mail. Third from the left is Fullerton Assistant Postmaster Charles Clark and at the extreme right is Fullerton Postmaster Richard S. Gregory who accompanied the mail flight.

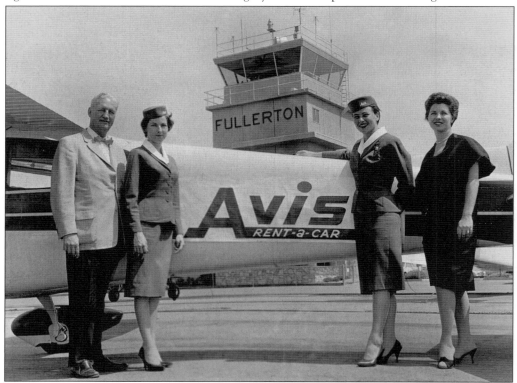

In 1958, the city's first Avis Rent-A-Car opened at the Fullerton Municipal Airport. Warren Avis had begun his company in 1946, opening his first outlets at Detroit's Willow Run Airport and Miami International Airport.

Seven

LIBRARIES, SCHOOLS, AND CHURCHES

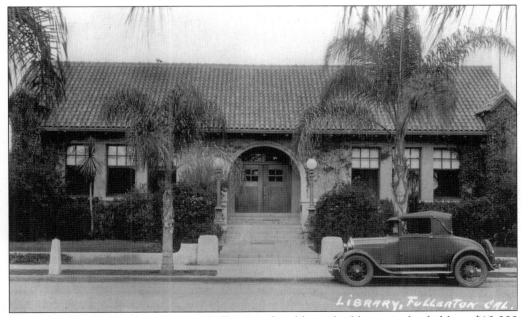

Located at North Pomona Avenue, Fullerton's first library building was funded by a $10,000 Andrew Carnegie grant. Constructed in 1907, the Mission/Spanish Colonial Revival building was razed in 1941 to make way for the new Work Projects Administration (WPA) library on the same spot. Flora Starbuck, whose Gem Pharmacy in 1888 housed the first books available to the public, was the first cardholder.

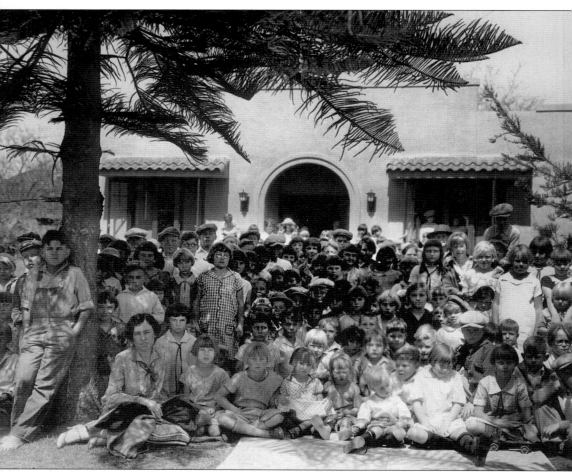

To alleviate a growing space problem, the Boys and Girls Library was added just west of the Carnegie library. Shown here on opening day on April 1, 1927, the children's annex was moved to Hillcrest Park at 1207 Lemon in 1941 to make way for the new WPA library. Children's librarian Mary Campbell, a seminal figure in Fullerton librarianship, is seated on the lower left. During her lifetime she developed one of the premier children's literature collections (the Mary Laura Campbell Collection), now housed in the main branch of the Fullerton Public Library.

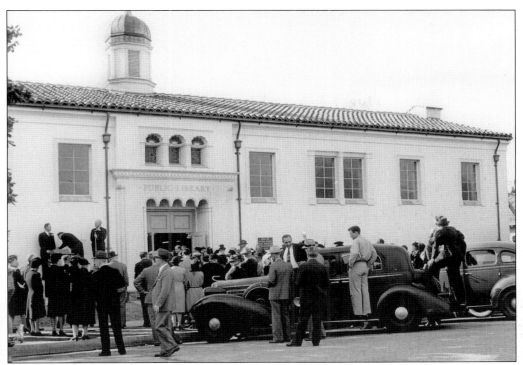

The Carnegie library was replaced by a new WPA library, shown here during dedication ceremonies held January 22–24, 1942. The library was designed by Harry Vaughn, a prominent architect who also designed the original Fullerton College campus. The building remains in use today as the Fullerton Museum Center at 301 North Pomona.

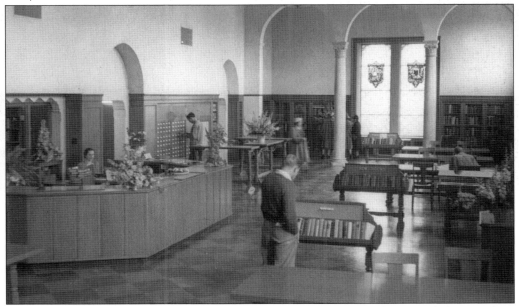

This photo shows the interior of the WPA library in the early 1940s. The stained-glass windows on the north wall were recently uncovered.

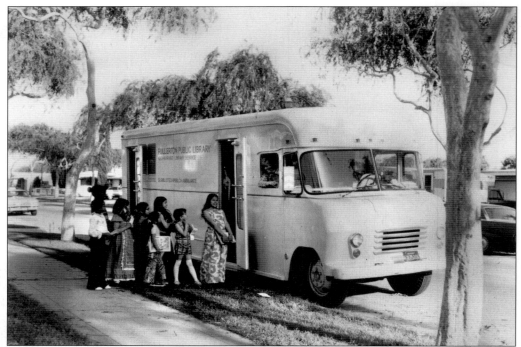

In 1957, Fullerton started the first bookmobile service in Orange County. Bookmobile librarian Barbara Weber, who connected readers with books for over 35 years, is shown here in 1973 at the Valencia and Lemon Avenues stop in Fullerton's second bookmobile.

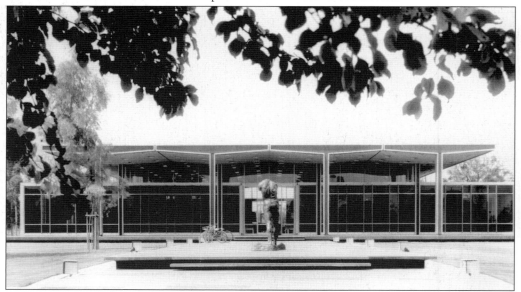

Built with a gift of $485,000 from the Hunt-Wesson Foundation, the Hunt Branch Library (1962) was designed by the renowned architect William Pereira. Norton Simon displayed his artwork, including the Auguste Rodin statute shown here, at the branch and hoped to build a museum nearby, but when an agreement with the city could not be reached, he moved his art collection to Pasadena.

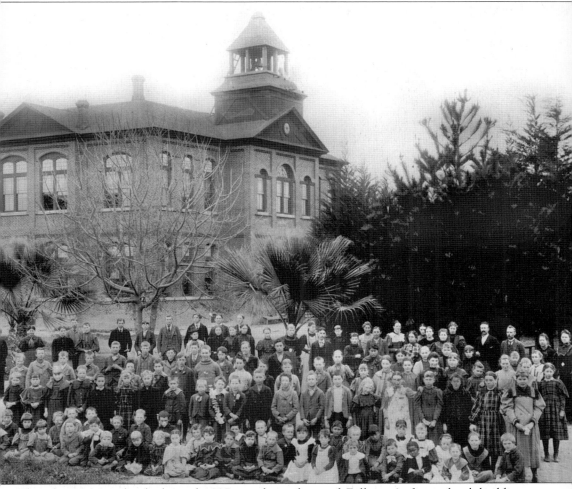

The elementary school class of 1897 stands in front of Fullerton's first school building, constructed in 1889. The brick building was located at East Wilshire and North Harvard (Lemon) Avenues. For a short time, the second floor was used for Fullerton High School.

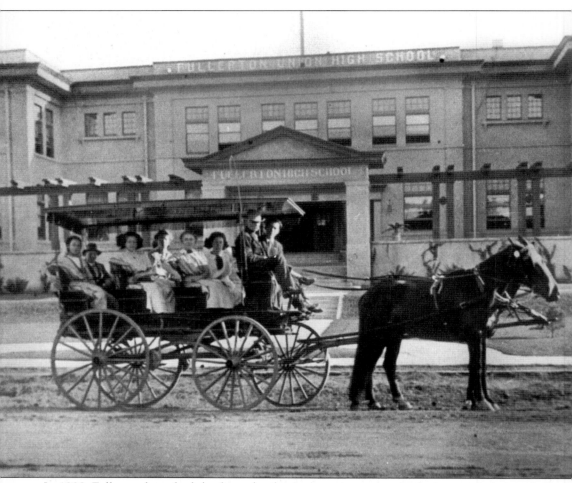

In 1908, Fullerton launched the first school transportation system in the state, consisting of six wagons that transported students to and from Fullerton High School. This new building in the 300 block of West Commonwealth was destroyed by a fire in 1910, and the high school moved to a new site on Chapman Avenue.

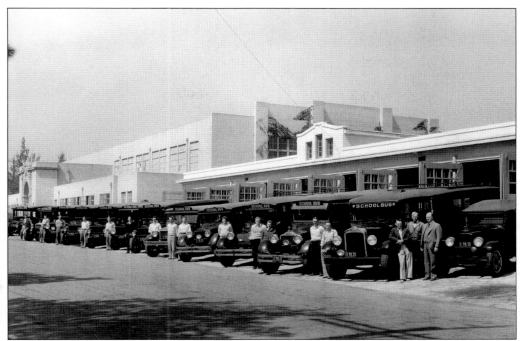

The horse-and-wagon school transportation system was later replaced by a motorized one, and by the early 1930s the district had a fleet of school buses. The buses, which served both the high school and Fullerton College, are shown here lined up along Pomona Avenue.

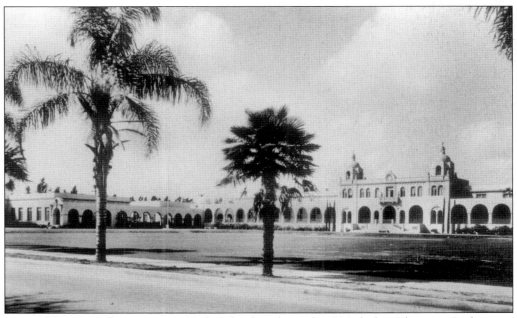

Pictured here is Fullerton Union High School in the early 1920s before Plummer Auditorium (1930) was constructed.

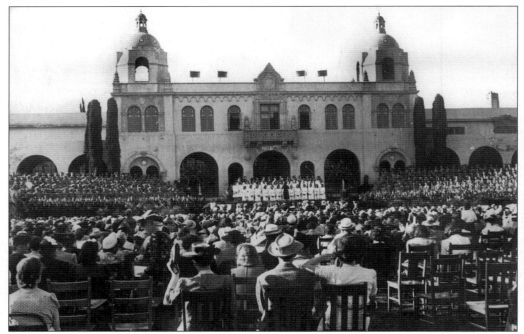

Commencements have always been a big draw for Fullerton residents, and this graduation ceremony held on the front lawn of Fullerton Union High School on June 19, 1941 was no exception.

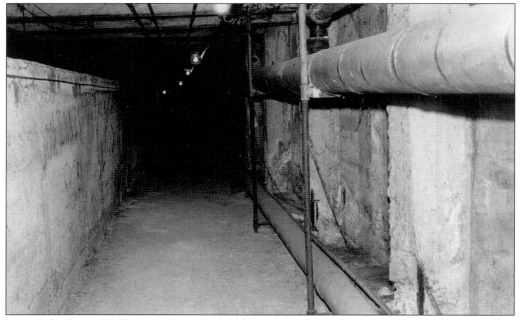

Part of the lore of Fullerton Union High School is the 2,000 feet of underground tunnels that connect most of the buildings on campus and reach under Lemon to Fullerton College. Constructed over 60 years ago, the tunnels were originally used for heating and pipelines, and later as a bomb shelter.

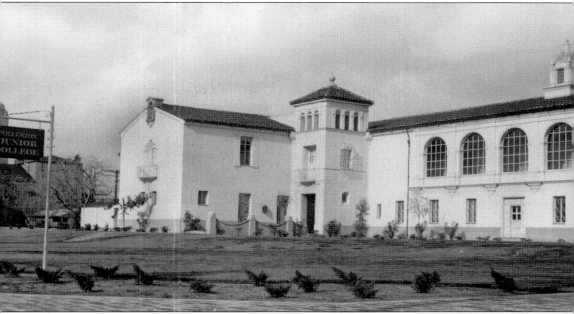

This photo shows Fullerton College in January 1942. Opened February 1913 to 28 students, it is the oldest continually operating community college in the state.

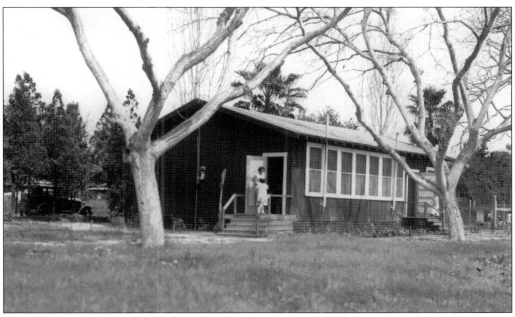

Known as the Ranch School, this one-room building on Bastanchury Ranch east of Fullerton Road served as a school for the children of 600 Mexican migrant worker families from 1927 to 1932. In 1933, it was moved to the Ford School grounds where it then served as a soup kitchen for the unemployed. The building is now located at the main offices of the Fullerton School District at 1401 West Valencia.

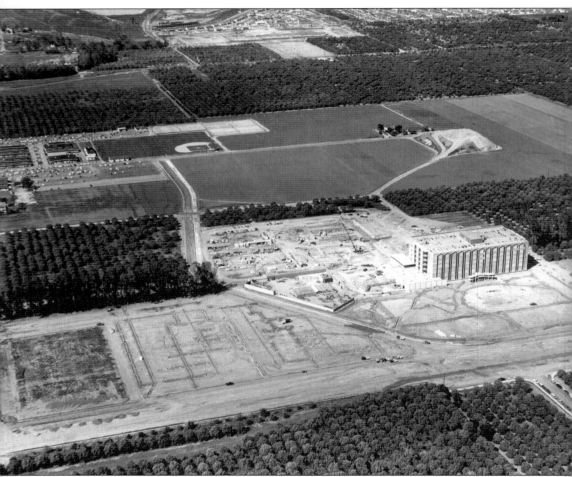

This April 1963 aerial photograph shows construction underway at Orange County State College, which became California State University, Fullerton in 1972. The small building on the top right is the brick Henry Hetebrink House (1886), the first building in the area, now known as the Titan House.

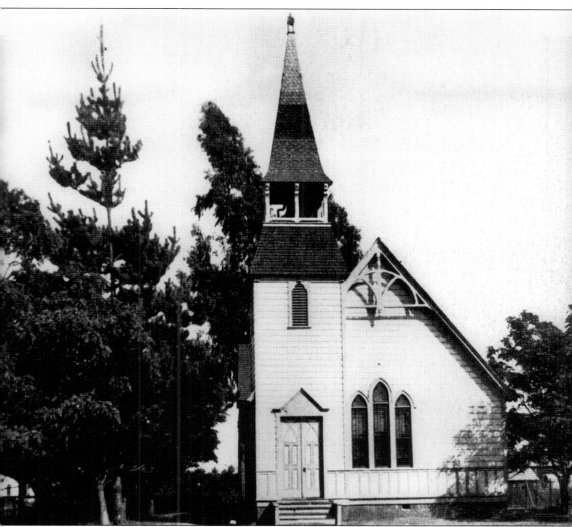

Dedicated June 30, 1889, this is Fullerton's first church, the First Presbyterian Church, located at the southeast corner of Pomona and Wilshire Avenues. The church was shared with the Baptist congregation, which later purchased the building, then demolished it to build a church of their own.

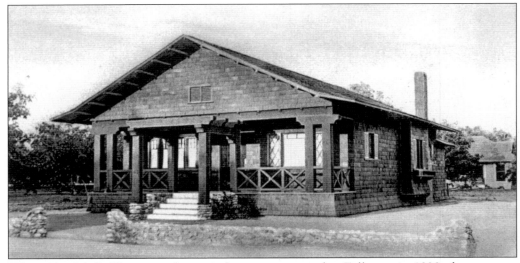

When Charles C. Chapman, the city's first mayor, moved to Fullerton in 1898, there was no First Christian Church so he attended a church in Anaheim. Looking forward to having a church in his hometown, Chapman purchased a lot in 1904 at the northeast corner of Spadra (Harbor) and Wilshire for the construction of a small chapel, which served as Fullerton's third church.

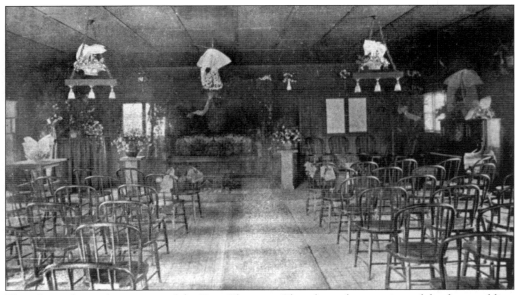

This photo shows the interior of the First Christian Church on the occasion of the first wedding held in the chapel on June 13, 1905, which united Luther Stull and Bessie Ellis. The congregation used the church until 1911, when it was moved to 115 East Brookdale, where it now stands.

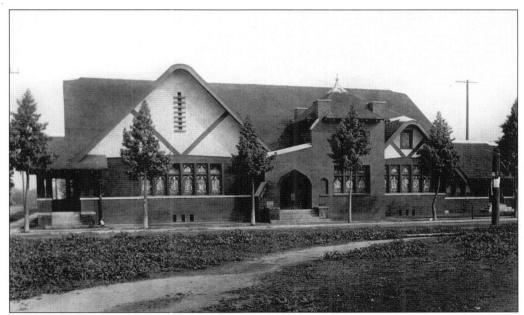

In 1911, the small Christian church was replaced with this brick veneer Tudor Revival church. The church, razed in 1971 to make way for the current First Christian Church building, was the only Tudor Revival–styled religious building in Fullerton.

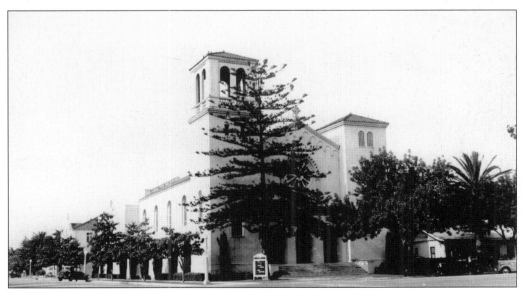

The First United Methodist Church was constructed in 1929 at a cost of $160,000, of which $130,000 was covered with five-year subscriptions. The Spanish Colonial Revival church at 114 North Pomona was designed by the noted architectural firm of Allison and Allison of Los Angeles, which specialized in large public buildings.

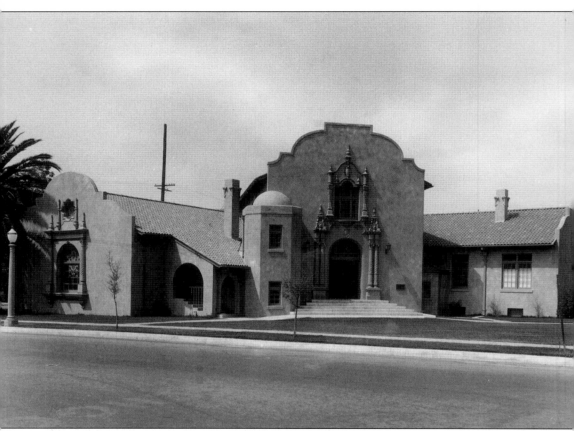

Erected in 1920, this Mission Revival structure was originally a Christian Science Church and is now the Self-Realization Fellowship Temple, located at 142 East Chapman. The temple's congregation follows the teachings of Paramahansa Yogananda (1893–1952), the first yoga master of India to take up permanent residence in the West. The elaborate relief decoration on the building's façade is unique to Fullerton.

Eight

CELEBRATIONS AND FAMOUS EVENTS

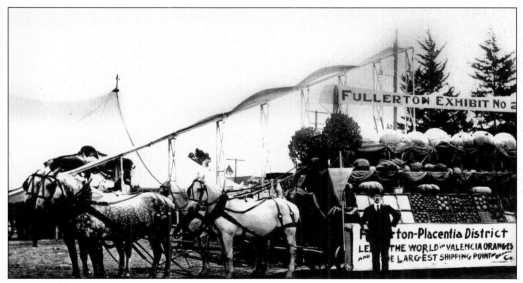

As agriculture became the dominant economic force in Fullerton, farmers and ranchers proudly displayed their produce and livestock at shows and fairs around the country, including the 1893 World's Columbian Exposition in Chicago. This photo of the Fullerton-Placentia District display was most likely taken at the time of the 1915 Panama-California Exposition in San Diego.

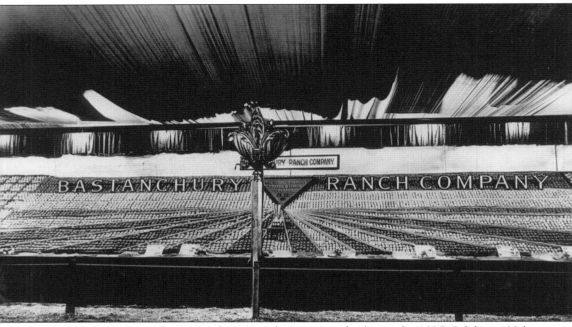

This photo features the Bastanchury Ranch Company display at the 1925 California Valencia Orange Show in Anaheim.

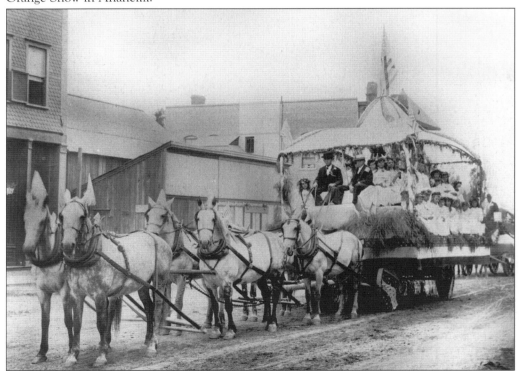

Fullerton residents started having parades down Spadra Road (now Harbor Boulevard) in the 1890s. Pictured here is a float in the 1897 Fourth of July parade.

Taken on West Amerige, this photo shows a float in the 1912 Fourth of July parade. The building is the original 1901 Masonic Temple at 201 North Harbor. The Masons used the second floor for meetings until the organization moved to its larger facility in 1919 at the northwest corner of Harbor Boulevard and Chapman Avenue.

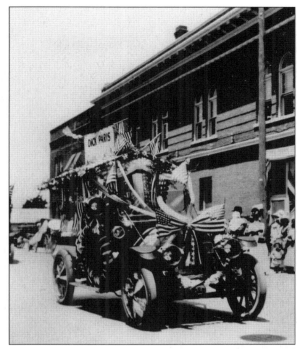

On October 2, 1946, over 6,000 people lined Spadra for the first annual Fall Festival Parade. Led by a color guard from the El Toro Marine Base, veterans from the Spanish-American War to World War II marched along with decorated cars, floats, bicycle riders, and horses. Additional festivities followed at Amerige Park.

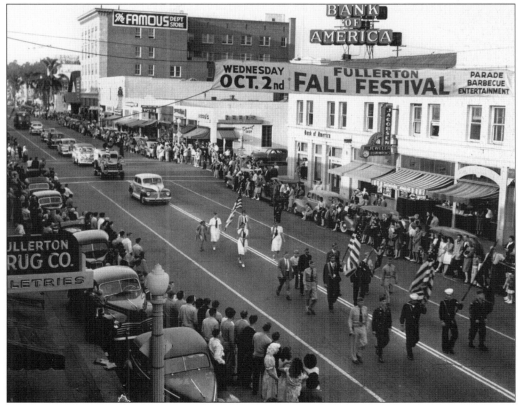

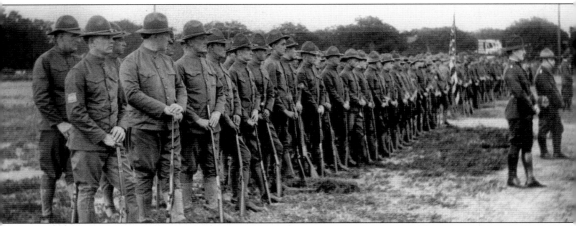

The Fullerton Home Guard was formed in 1917 in response to World War I. The volunteers, who had purchased their own uniforms and guns, drilled each Monday night in Amerige Park. Many of the militiamen shown here went on to fight in France. On May 12, 1898, an earlier Fullerton Home Guard of 72 members was formed in response to the Spanish-American War.

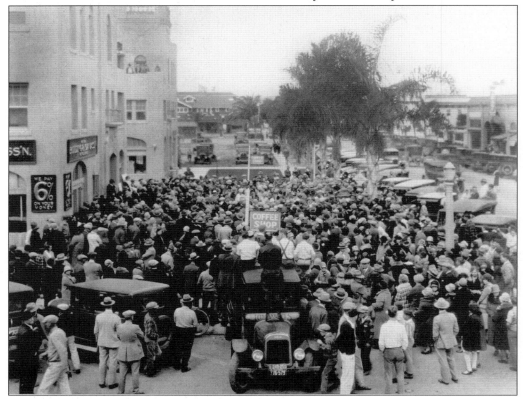

On January 15, 1923, Fullerton residents flocked to the grand opening of the California Hotel (now Villa del Sol), built with funds raised by public subscription. The three-story building contained 22 apartments and 55 hotel rooms with some shops on the ground floor. The hotel quickly became *the* place to stay when visiting the area, and the *Fullerton News Tribune* published regular reports on who was registered there.

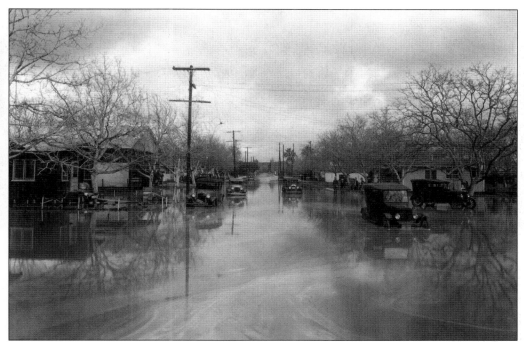

On New Year's Day 1900, Fullerton experienced its first flood, which claimed the life of blacksmith James Gardiner and left the downtown area under 8 to 12 inches of water. Floods continued to intermittently batter the town for the next 40 years. Looking north from the south end of Balcom Avenue around 10 a.m., this photo shows the flood of February 9, 1932.

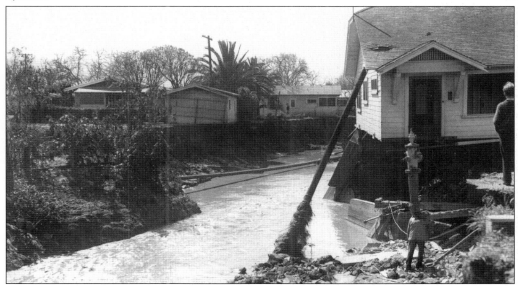

On March 3, 1938, the largest flood on record swept through the city. This photo of East Brookdale Place shows Brea Creek flowing unchecked through the area. After this devastating flood, city officials used Depression-era government relief funds to construct flood control channels.

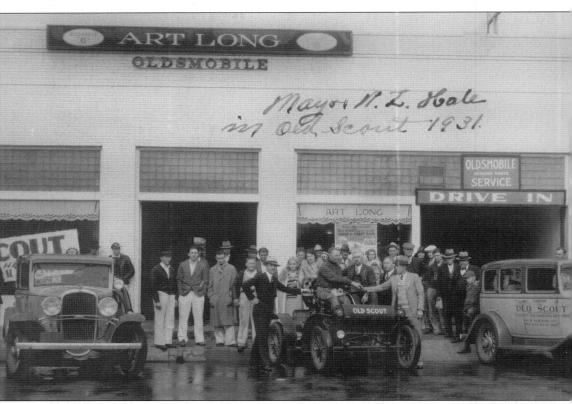

In 1905, Old Scout, a 1902 Oldsmobile Roundabout, won the first transcontinental race, crossing the country in 44 days and proving beyond all doubt that the automobile could provide dependable transportation. Twenty-six years later, the Olds repeated the route, visiting dealerships along the way, including a stop at Art Long Oldsmobile at 131 West Commonwealth. Over 10 million people came out to inspect the car during its "Now on Good Roads Tour."

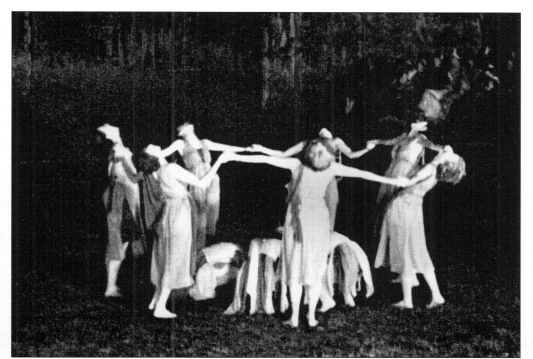

As part of Fullerton's Golden Jubilee Celebration, Fullerton Union High School staged an elaborate pageant May 13–15, 1937 that included 14 episodes devoted to the city's history. Shown here is episode 1, "The Land of Flowers Comes to Life," which featured a creation ballet.

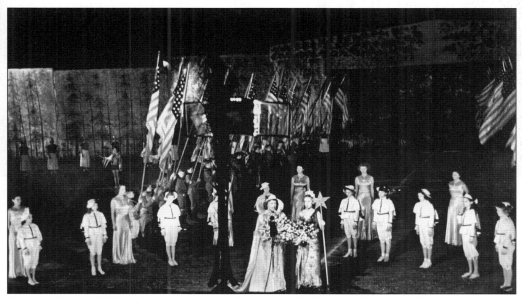

Pearl McCauley Philips (center with tiara), queen of Fullerton's Golden Jubilee Celebration, stands with members of her court, which included Mary Catherine Morgan (with star) as Miss Columbia and 48 other women, each representing a state. The selection of Mrs. Philips as Fullerton's golden anniversary queen was controversial at the time because she was married.

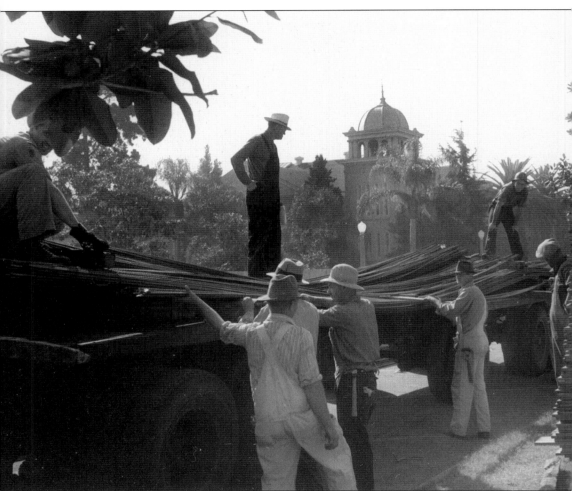

During the Depression, Fullerton applied for and received more federal relief funds than any other city in Orange County. In this 1940 photo, WPA workers are constructing the new city library on North Pomona. In the background is the First Baptist Church (1912) designed by Frederick Eley (1884–1979), Orange County's first architect. Eley designed over 125 buildings in the county, including the Fullerton General Hospital at 201 East Amerige.

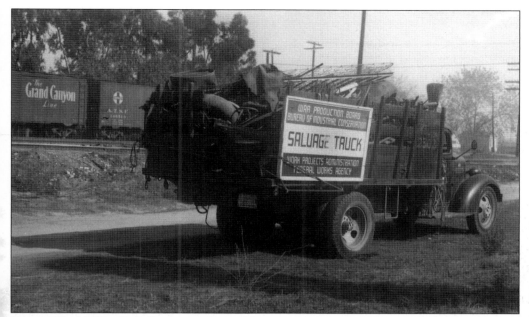

During World War II, Fullerton residents, like other Americans, were asked to salvage a long list of materials for the war effort, including paper, tin, iron, rubber, and even silk stockings and cooking fat. This 1942 photo shows a government salvage truck parked next to Fullerton's railroad tracks.

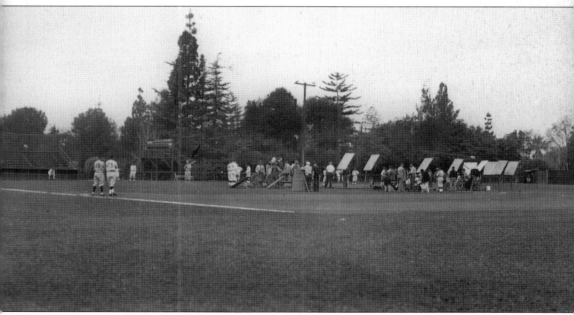

Fullerton residents came out in March 1935 to watch filming of the comedy *Alibi Ike* in Amerige Park. Star Joe E. Brown (left center with bat) briefly played semiprofessional ball. Other movies filmed in Fullerton include *Purple People Eater* (1988), *Criminal Art* (1989), *Dr. Caligari* (1989), *Dreamrider* (1993), *Touch* (1997), *Evolution* (2001), *Mothman* (2000), and *Waking Up in Reno* (2002).

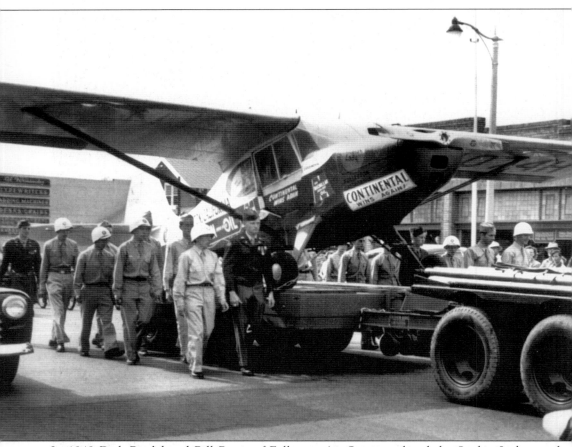

In 1949 Dick Riedel and Bill Barris of Fullerton Air Service piloted the *Sunkist Lady*, a red and white converted Aeronca, into the endurance flight record books by staying aloft 1,008 hours and 2 minutes—a total of 42 days. They were welcomed home in a grand parade down Commonwealth Avenue and up Spradra Road.

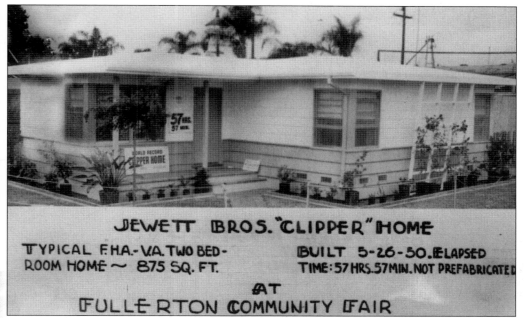

JEWETT BROS. "CLIPPER" HOME

TYPICAL F.H.A.-V.A. TWO BED-
ROOM HOME ~ 875 SQ. FT.

BUILT 5-26-50. ELAPSED
TIME: 57 HRS. 57 MIN. NOT PREFABRICATED

AT
FULLERTON COMMUNITY FAIR

On May 25, 1970, the Jewett Brothers Construction Company set a world record by constructing a two-bedroom tract home in 57 hours and 57 minutes.

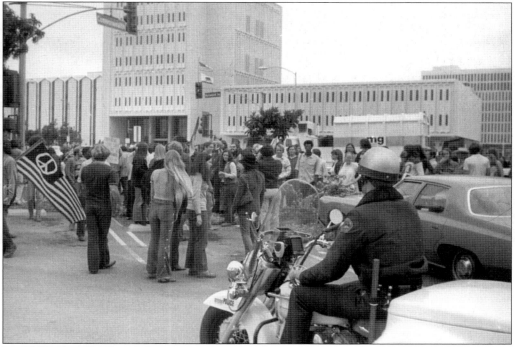

In 1969, the California State University, Fullerton campus (then Orange County State College) was the well-publicized site of anti-war demonstrations during the Vietnam War. This photo shows police and students in front of Langsdorf Hall, the campus administration building, on Nutwood Avenue.

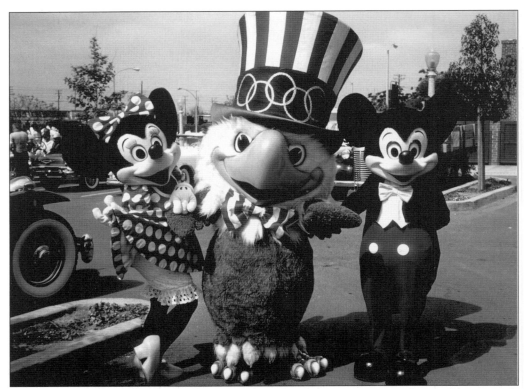

On July 26, 1984, thousands of Fullerton residents lined the streets to watch a torchbearer with the Olympic flame run down Harbor Boulevard. A few days later, CSU Fullerton hosted the Olympic team handball competition. In this photo, Minnie and Mickey Mouse pose with Sam the Eagle (the Los Angeles Olympic Games mascot) at the Transportation Center. Sam was designed by the Walt Disney Company. (Photo courtesy of Terry Galvin.)

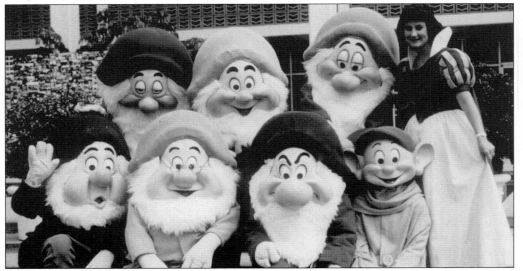

Snow White and the Seven Dwarves pose in front of Fullerton City Hall in 1987 to celebrate Fullerton's 100th anniversary. (Photo courtesy of Terry Galvin.)

Nine

BUILDINGS ON THE NATIONAL REGISTER OF HISTORIC PLACES

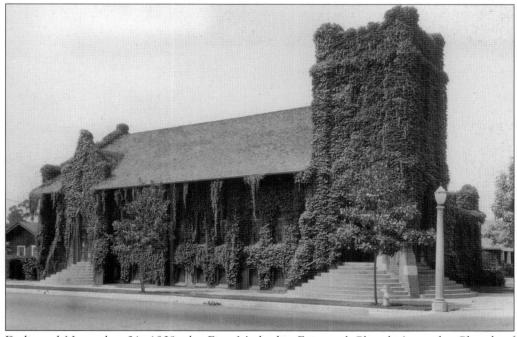

Dedicated November 21, 1909, the First Methodist Episcopal Church (now the Church of Religious Science), shown here in 1927, is the finest example of Gothic Revival architecture in Fullerton and the oldest continuous church in the city. Located at 117 North Pomona, the building's Simons Company bricks, opalescent glass, and stained-glass windows are unique to Fullerton. Master builder Albert R. Walker (1881–1959) designed the church, as well as over 300 other buildings in California.

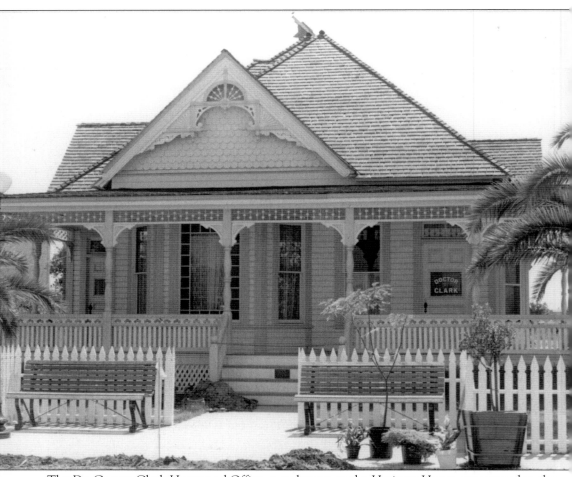

The Dr. George Clark House and Office, now known as the Heritage House, was moved to the Fullerton Arboretum from its original location at 114 North Lemon in 1972 and carefully restored. Built in the Victorian Eastlake style in 1894 for $1,300, the Clark House is one of the oldest surviving homes constructed within the city's original townsite. Dr. Clark was one of the most highly regarded individuals in Fullerton. He served on the first city council in 1904, was instrumental in having the Fullerton General Hospital constructed in 1913, and brought into the world over 2,500 Orange Countians.

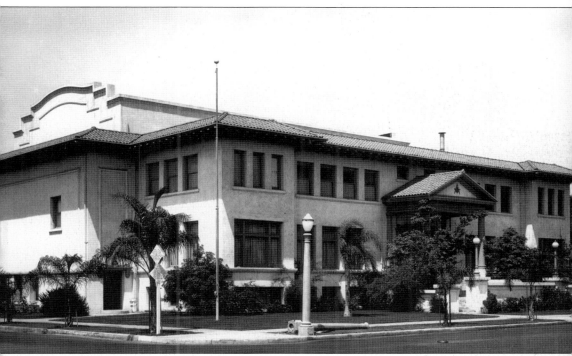

When Fullerton's Masonic Order outgrew its original quarters at 201 North Harbor, it built this Spanish Colonial Revival meeting hall at the corner of Harbor Boulevard and Chapman Avenue in 1919. The Masonic Temple soon became the center of social activities and charitable events in Fullerton. In 1995, the current owner restored the building, now known as the Spring Field Banquet and Conference Center.

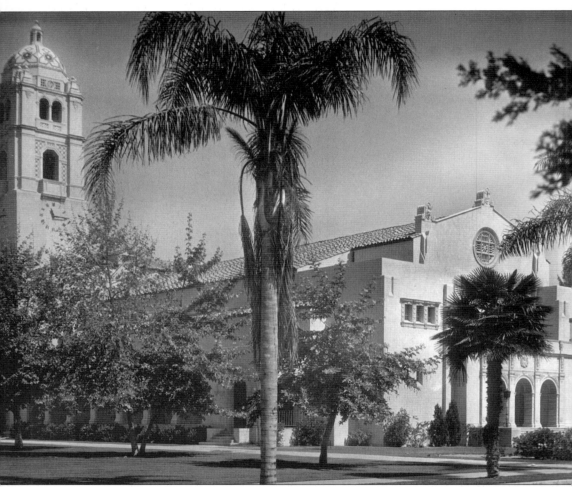

Designed by architect Carlton M. Winslow and constructed for $295,500 in 1930, the Plummer Auditorium at 201 East Chapman is an outstanding example of Spanish Colonial Revival architecture with Italian Renaissance design elements. The building, shown here in 1934, is named for Louis E. Plummer, superintendent of Fullerton High School and Fullerton Junior College from 1919 to 1941.

Plummer Auditorium, which seats 1,300 people, features an elaborate ceiling of painted and decorated rough-hewn beams, the original wrought-iron chandeliers, and other classical ornamentation. The grand Wurlitzer organ, original to the building, was restored and is in use today.

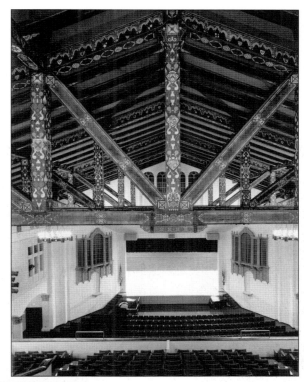

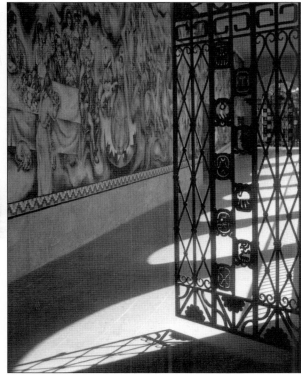

This 1934 photo shows "Pastoral California," a 75-foot by 15-foot mural painted on the west side of Plummer Auditorium by WPA artist Charles Kassler. The fresco was painted over in 1939, then totally restored through a community effort in 1997. A landmark in its own right, the mural is a vivid picture of California history in the early 1800s.

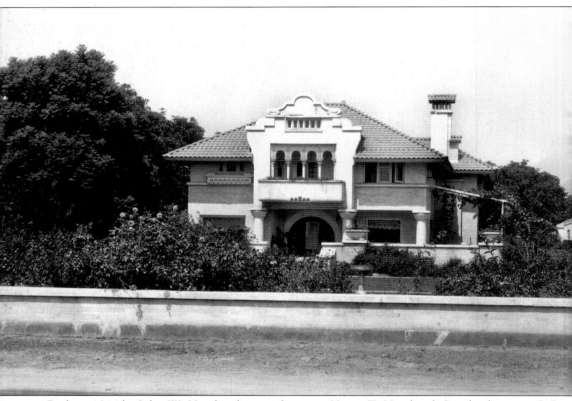

Built in 1914 by John W. Hetebrink, son of pioneer Henry T. Hetebrink Sr., this house at 515 East Chapman is the most outstanding example of Mission Revival architecture in Fullerton. John Hetebrink became a successful farmer who made his own fortune in the tomato, walnut, and citrus industries. The house was once part of a 40-acre ranch north of Chapman Avenue.

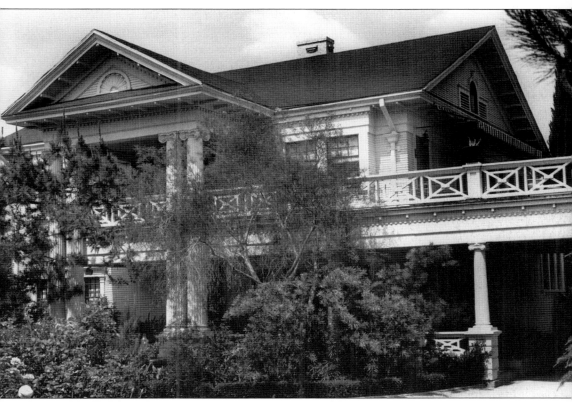

Built by the Pierotti family in 1909, this home at 1731 North Bradford is the finest example of the Neoclassical style in Fullerton. Surrounded by about one acre of gardens and an orchard, it is the only remaining estate from the pre-1910 era to survive intact in its original setting in north Orange County.

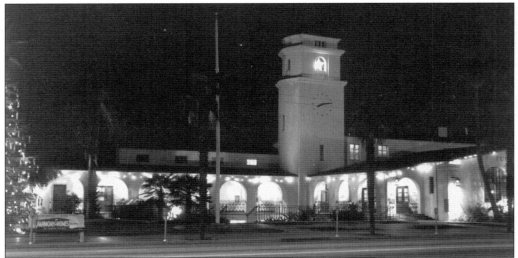

An exceptionally fine example of the Spanish Colonial Revival style applied to civic architecture, the Fullerton City Hall at 237 West Commonwealth, now the police station, was built with WPA funds from 1939 to 1942. The building's architect was G. Stanley Wilson (1879–1958), an acknowledged master of Spanish styles, who also designed much of the famed Riverside Mission Inn.

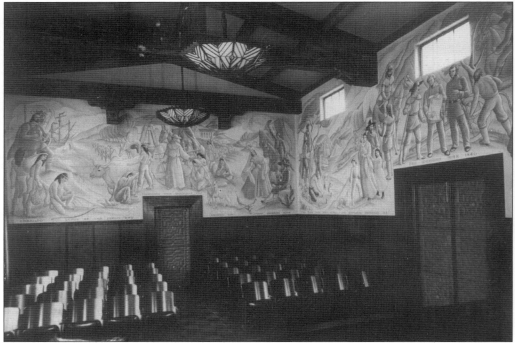

The former Fullerton City Hall houses a valuable art treasure: a series of murals depicting Southern California history painted by famed artist Helen Lundeberg (1908–1999). Titled "The History of Southern California," the panorama of panels depicts early California history from the landing of Juan Rodriguez Cabrillo at San Diego Bay in 1542 to the early days of the movie industry in Hollywood.

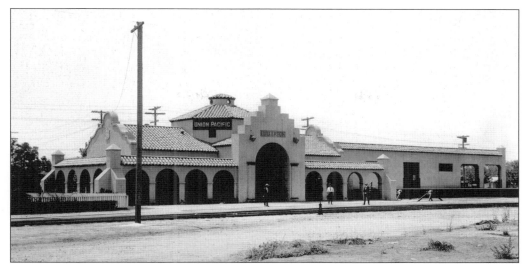

The Union Pacific was the last of the three railroads to come to Fullerton, completing work on the company's depot in 1923. The City Redevelopment Agency, recognizing the historical significance of the building, purchased the depot in 1980, saving it from demolition, and moved it from the 100 block of West Truslow to its current location at the Transportation Center.

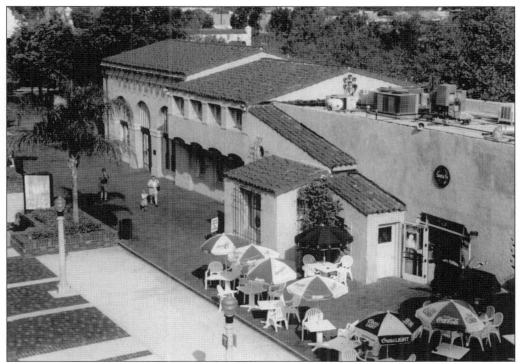

Built in 1930, the present Santa Fe Depot replaced the original Victorian depot that was constructed in 1888, a year after the arrival of the railroad in Fullerton. Since 1930, and particularly during the 1940s, the depot has been the first building people see when they arrive in Fullerton by train.

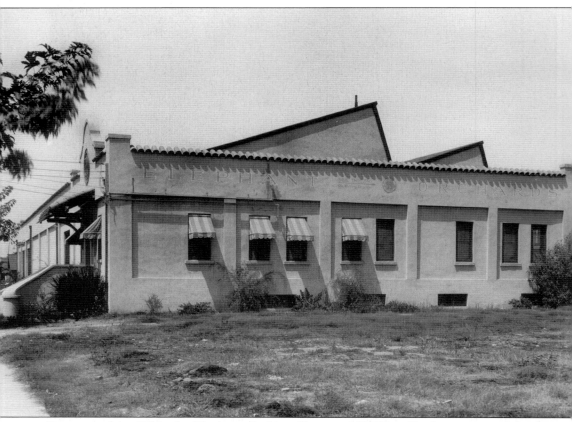

Constructed in 1914, the Elephant Packing Plant at 201 West Truslow is one of the last remaining packinghouses in Fullerton, where at one time as many as ten such plants lined the railroad tracks. It was originally leased to Elephant Orchards of Redlands, but in 1932 the Chapman family subleased the facility and for over 20 years the Chapmans' Old Mission Brand Valencia oranges were packed here.

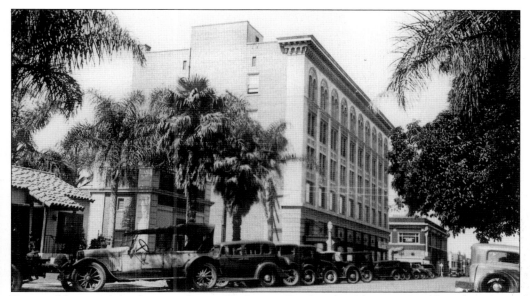

Designed by noted Anaheim architect M. Eugene Durfee, the Chapman Building at 110 East Wilshire is Fullerton's most outstanding commercial structure. Built for Charles Chapman, Fullerton's first mayor, the structure's 65-foot height was the tallest in Orange County when erected in 1923. It housed the area's first department store, including the Chapman-Wickett Company, Ferber's, and Famous.

The construction of the Chapman Building was an enormous project, costing over $300,000 and requiring the services of 13 different local contractors. The building's steel skeletal frame, still a relatively new form of construction, made the brick building's height possible. In the background is Charles C. Chapman's church, the First Christian Church.

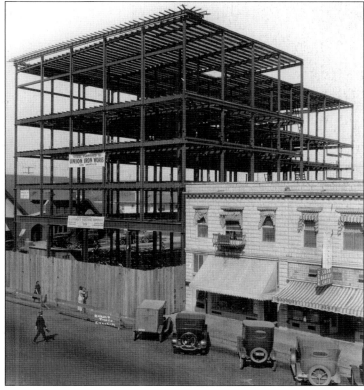

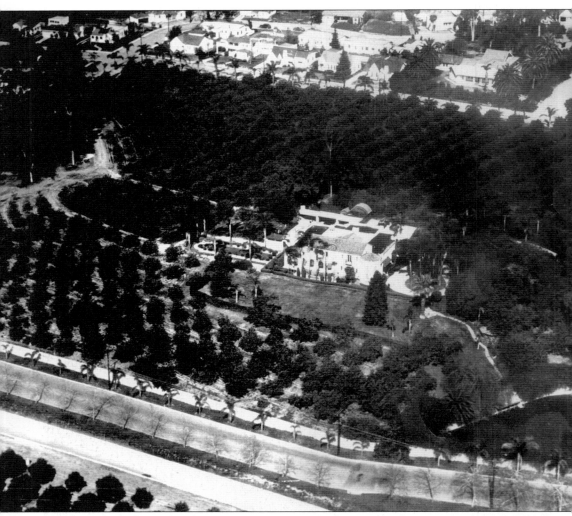

The Muckenthaler Cultural Center at 1201 West Malvern is the former estate home of Adella and Walter Muckenthaler. The 85-acre property where the house and grounds are located was granted to the city in 1965, with the stipulation that it be used as a cultural center. The house is one of the most significant Orange County examples of Mediterranean residential architecture. It was designed by Frank Benchley, who also designed the California Hotel, the second Masonic Temple, the Pomona Bungalow Court, and the Farmers and Merchants Bank.

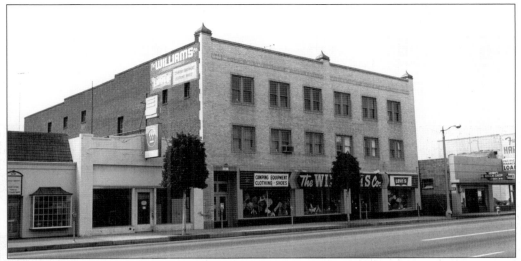

The Fullerton Odd Fellows Temple (now the Williams Company) was constructed in 1927–1928 for one of the city's oldest fraternal organizations, the Independent Order of Odd Fellows Lodge No. 103 (1901–1981). Over the decades, dozens of patriotic, fraternal, and women's organizations used the temple, located at 112 East Commonwealth, for meetings, including veterans of the Civil and Spanish-American Wars.

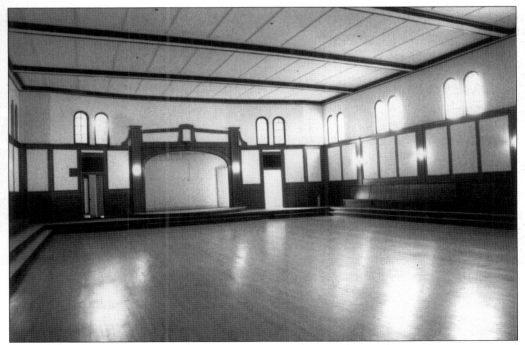

The focal point of the interior of the Odd Fellows Temple is the large second-floor meeting and assembly hall (known as the Hall of Truth), shown here in 2001, which featured a stage, built-in tiered seating on the sides, and high, arched windows. (Photo courtesy of Kathryn Morris.)

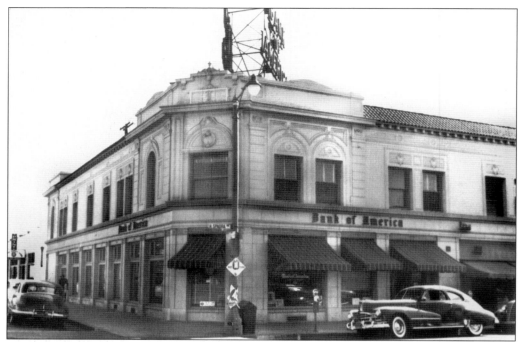

Although built in 1904, the Farmers and Merchants Bank at 122 North Harbor received its richly detailed Beaux-Arts façade in a 1922 redesign by local architect Frank Benchley. The prominent two-story building is the only example of the Beaux-Arts style in Fullerton. The Farmers and Merchants Bank was the forerunner to the Bank of Italy and later the Bank of America.

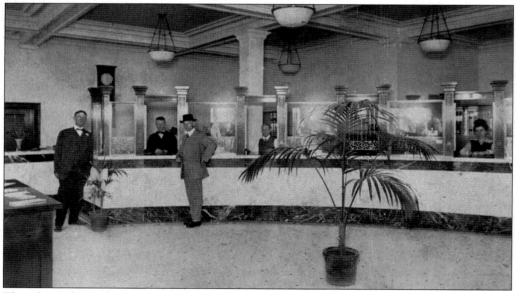

This photo shows the interior of the Farmers and Merchants Bank in the 1920s.

Ten

ODDS AND ENDS

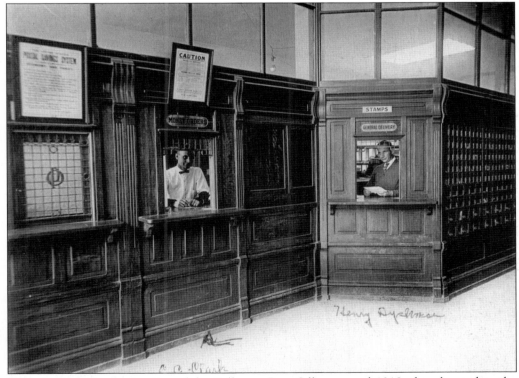

This photo shows the interior of the Fullerton Post Office around 1918, then located in the Farmers and Merchants Bank. Postal clerk Charles Clark is on the left; mail carrier Henry Dyckman is on the right.

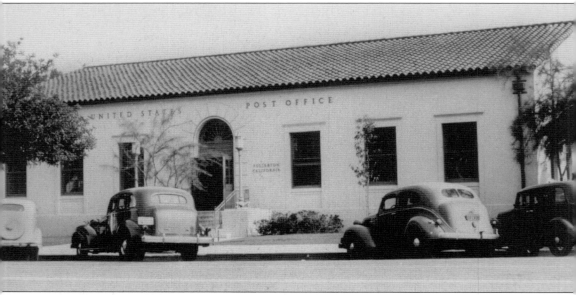

Constructed by the federal government for $56,000 in less than seven months, Fullerton's first post office building at 202 East Commonwealth was dedicated on November 1, 1938. The interior features a WPA mural, known for its historical inaccuracies, painted by Illinois native Paul Julian.

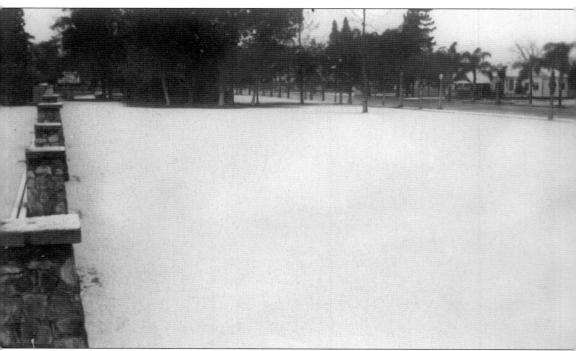

After a freak snow on January 11, 1949, the heaviest snow storm on record, snow covered Amerige Park. A white blanket from a half-inch to two inches thick covered the Orange County area from the beaches to the foothills.

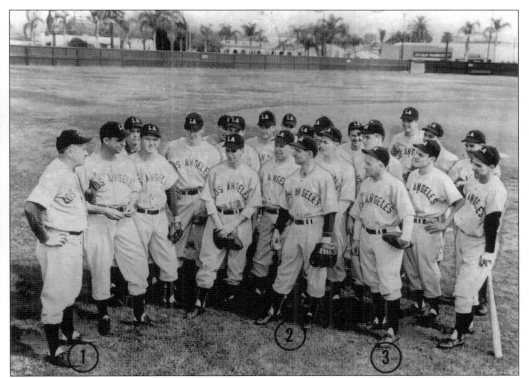

This photo shows the opening of the spring training camp for the Los Angeles Angels at Amerige Park in 1949, with (1) manager Bill Kelley, (2) coach Jackie Warner, and (3) coach Jigger Statz. The team was a member of the Pacific Coast League from 1925 to 1957. (Photo courtesy of the Herald Examiner Collection, Los Angeles Public Library.)

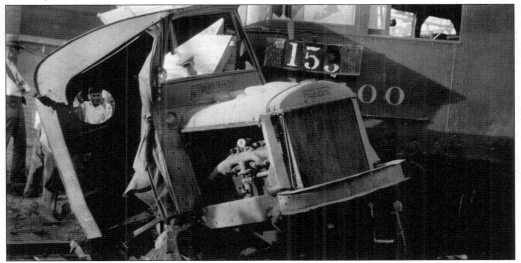

On September 16, 1925, William F. Hetebrink Jr., Fullerton's street department foreman, was killed in this collision of a city dump truck and a Union Pacific passenger car at the South Harvard (Lemon) Avenue crossing. Hetebrink was the first Fullerton city employee to die in an on-the-job accident.

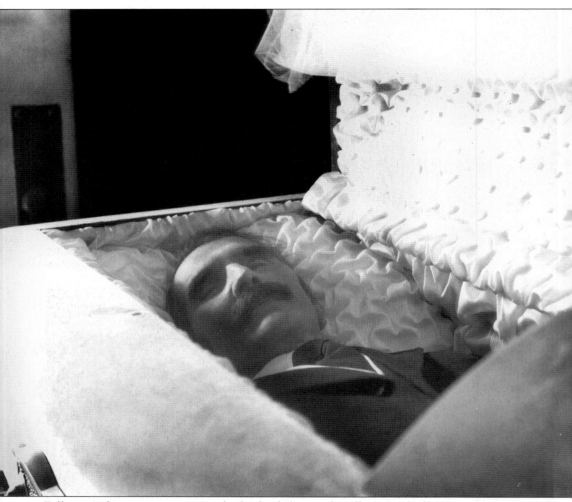

Fullerton's first mortuary was in the back of Flora and William Starbuck's Gem Pharmacy, but by the late 1890s funeral homes, such as Lippincott's, had become established on Spadra Road. This photo shows an unidentified Fullerton resident laid out to rest in the 1890s.

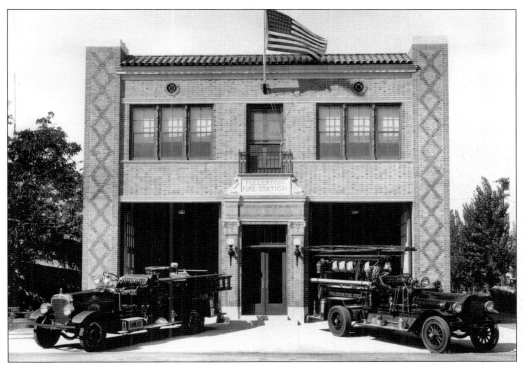

Until 1926, when Fullerton's first fire station was built, firemen and their equipment were stationed in a series of rundown sheds. Located on Wilshire Avenue, the two-story building shown here also housed city offices until 1942 when Fullerton's first city hall (now the police station) was built.

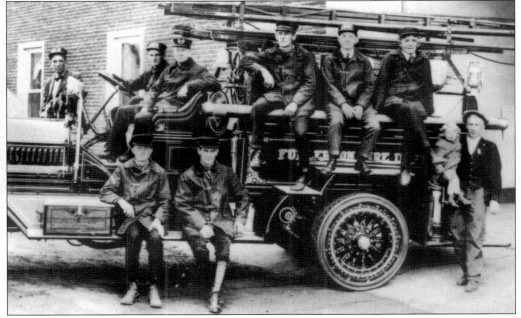

In this 1926 photo, Fullerton firemen show off their new equipment.

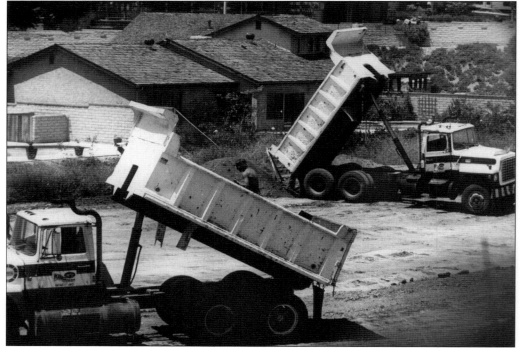

This 1997 photo shows the clean-up of the McColl dump site, one of the most toxic waste sites in the nation at the time. Located on Rosecrans Avenue, the 22-acre site, owned by Ely McColl, was used as a dumping ground for refinery wastes from 1942 to 1946, later endangering the health of those living in adjacent residential developments.

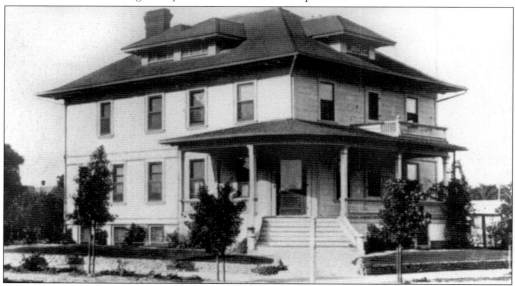

Fullerton's first hospital was constructed in 1903 and later demolished to make way for another hospital built on the same site. Charles C. Chapman was chairman of the board of directors, which included C.L. Rich, B.C. Balcom, William Starbuck, Dr. Willliam Freeman, Dr. D.W. Hansen, and Dr. George C. Clark.

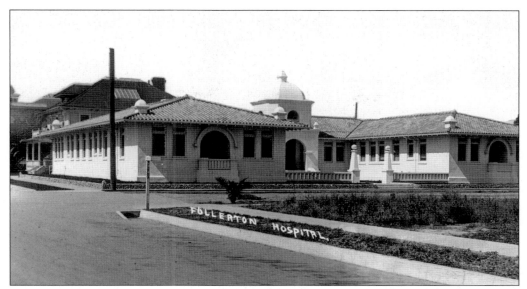

Constructed in 1915 and designed by Frederick Eley, Orange County's first architect, Fullerton's second hospital at 201 East Amerige is now owned by a private social service agency.

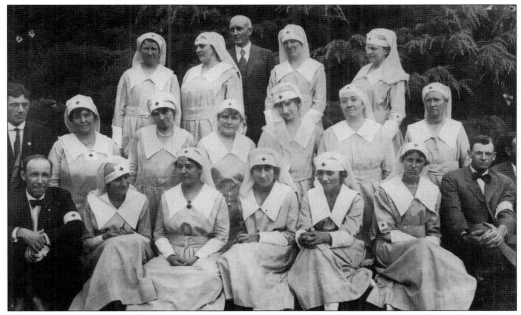

This postcard shows Fullerton Red Cross workers around 1917.

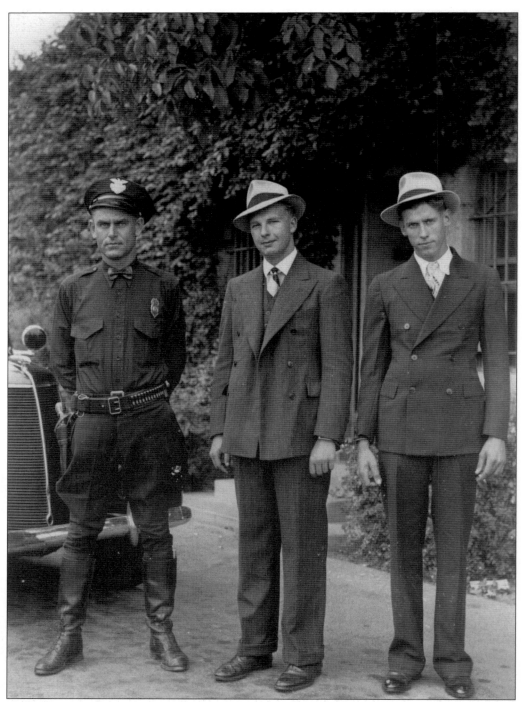

On September 17, 1937 at 7 a.m., bank robbers George Horine and William B. Morrison overturned their car after hitting a culvert at Spadra Road and Whiting Avenue. The two men, who had robbed the Saratoga Bank of America near San Jose of $760 four days earlier, were each sentenced to five years in San Quentin.

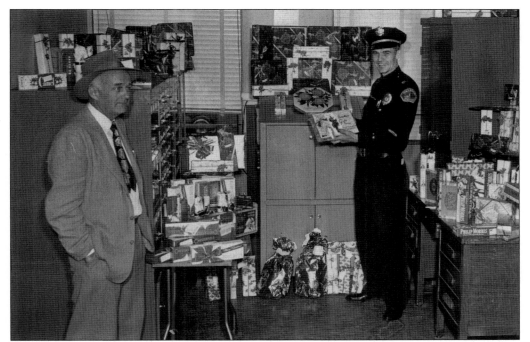

This photo shows the Fullerton Police Station at Christmastime in 1952.

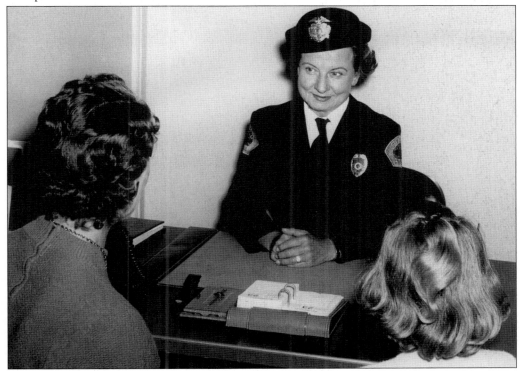

Pictured here is Geraldine Kelley Gregory, Fullerton's first female police officer. She was hired in 1959 primarily to work with adult females and juveniles.

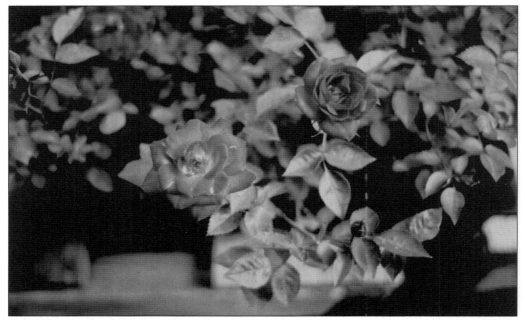

The Fullerton Rose, a hybrid flower, was developed for the city's centennial. Fullerton's official flower is the carnation. The official tree is the jacaranda.

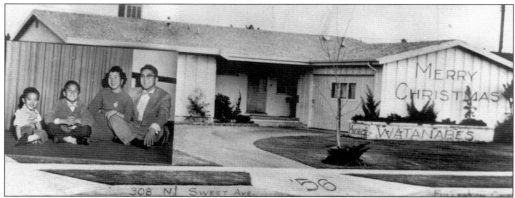

These Christmas greetings are from Ikudo and Hideo Watanabe and their two children from their home on Sweet Avenue in 1956. Hideo was then a chemist at Beckman Instruments. (Photo courtesy of Shades of L.A. Archives, Los Angeles Public Library.)

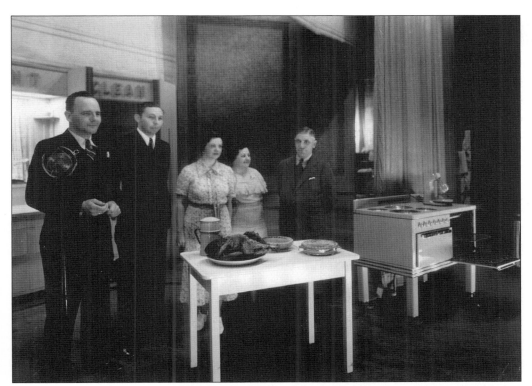

Before infomercials, Fullerton residents were treated to free product demonstrations. In this photo, Edison Company officials (left) show off a new electric stove at the Fox Fullerton Theatre in the early 1930s.

On August 18, 1960, the once stately Charles Chapman mansion at 110 North Cypress was destroyed by arsonists . Completed in 1903, the three-story house was the largest dwelling in Orange County when it was built. At the time of the fire, a new development, Chapman Park Homes, was under construction at the original ranch site.

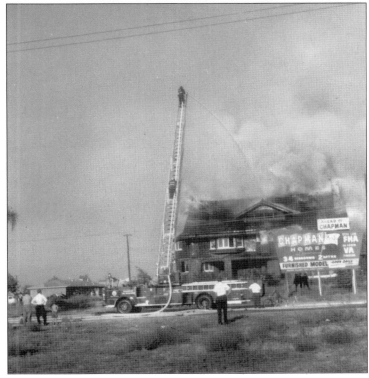

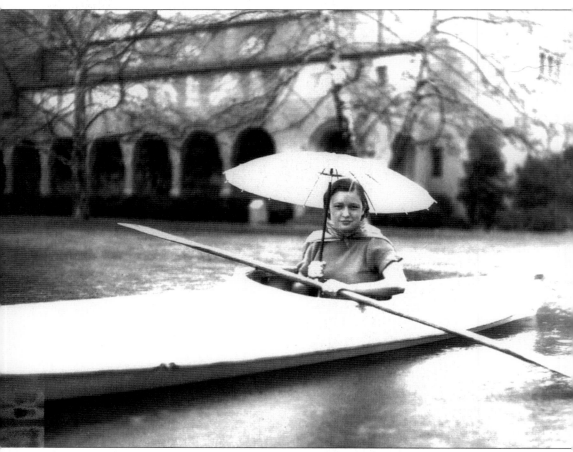

This photo shows a member of the Fullerton College Kayak Club during the 1938 flood.

For 38 years the Dames de Caridad (Ladies of Charity) sponsored Bal Masque, a floral-headdress ball that raised money for the St. Jude Medical Center. This photo shows the 1984 first place sweepstakes winner "In Another Galaxy Far Away," featuring Karen Gallio and Scott Acevedo.

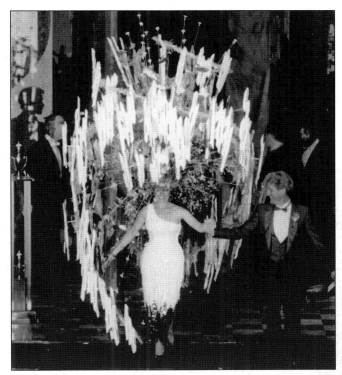

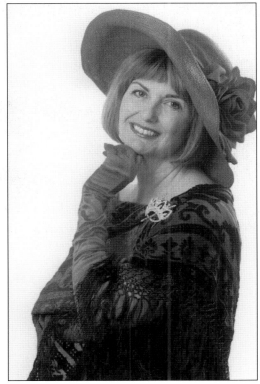

In 1998, Sue Ellen Cooper formed the founding chapter of the Red Hat Society in Fullerton with an afternoon tea. RHS, which offers fun and friendship to women over age 50, now has 600,000 members and 25,000 chapters in 21 countries. (Photo courtesy of the Red Hat Society.)

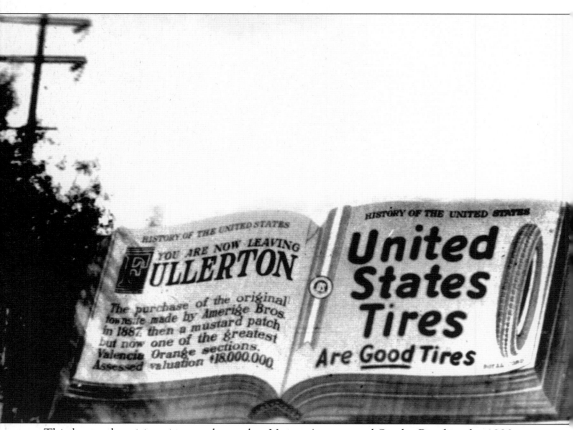

This large advertising sign was located at Union Avenue and Spadra Road in the 1920s.